ronin

the art of
christopher shy

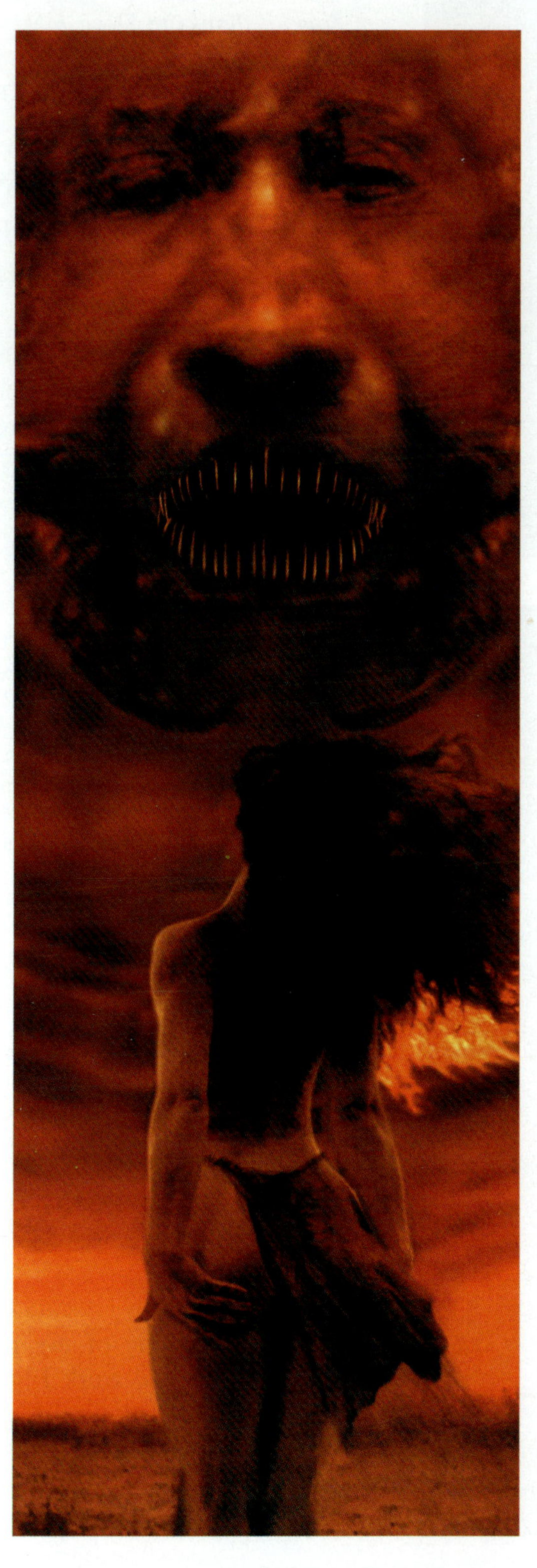

1

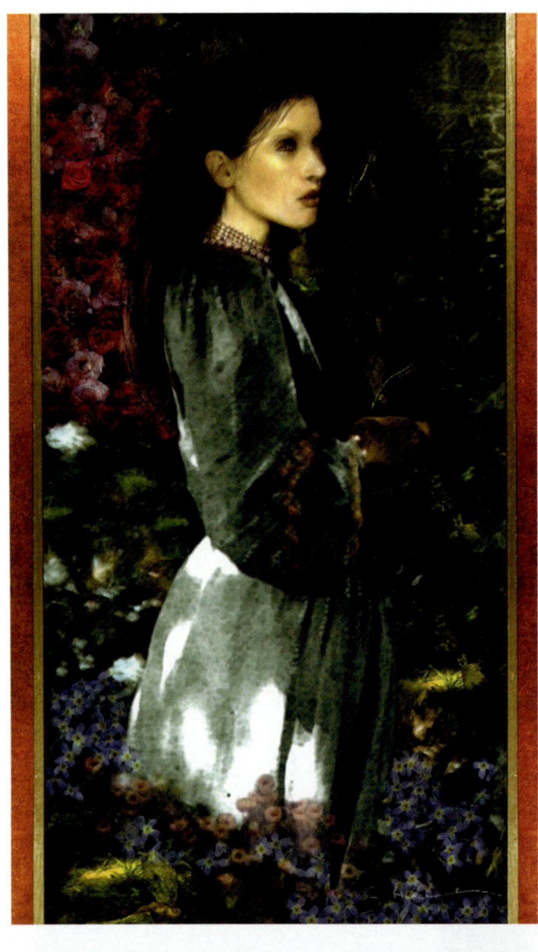

ronin
the art of christopher shy

Dedicated to my son, Alexander Shy.
Special thanks to Steve Jackson, Philip Reed, and Rich Thomas.

Commentary by Christopher Shy
Introduction by Kenneth Hite
Proofreading by Andrew Hackard
Book coordination, design,
and production by Philip Reed

Editor in Chief ✠ Steve Jackson
Managing Editor ✠ Alain H. Dawson
Production Manager ✠ Gene Seabolt
Print Buyer ✠ Paul Rickert
Art Director ✠ Philip Reed
Sales Manager ✠ Ross Jepson

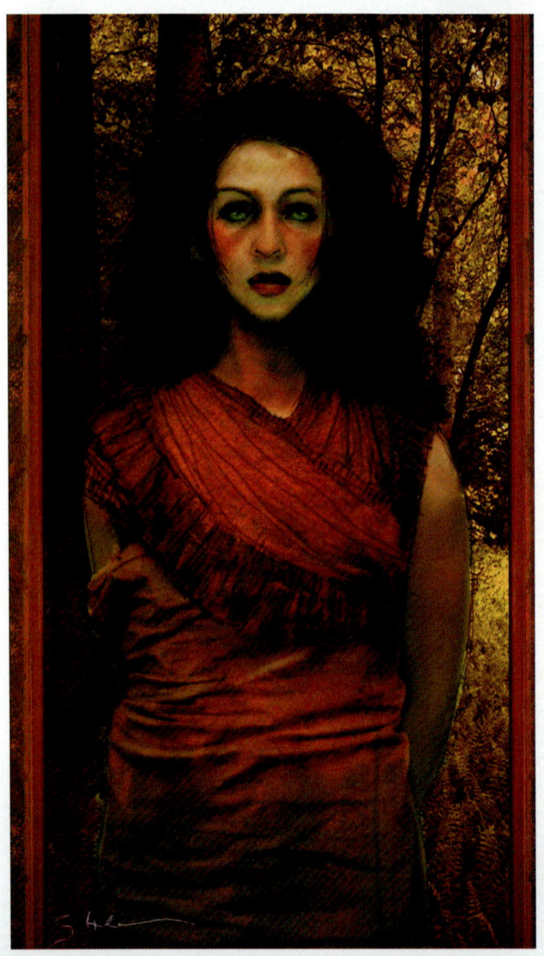

Cartouche Press is a trademark of Steve Jackson Games Incorporated.

ISBN 1-55634-546-1   1 2 3 4 5 6 7 8 9 10

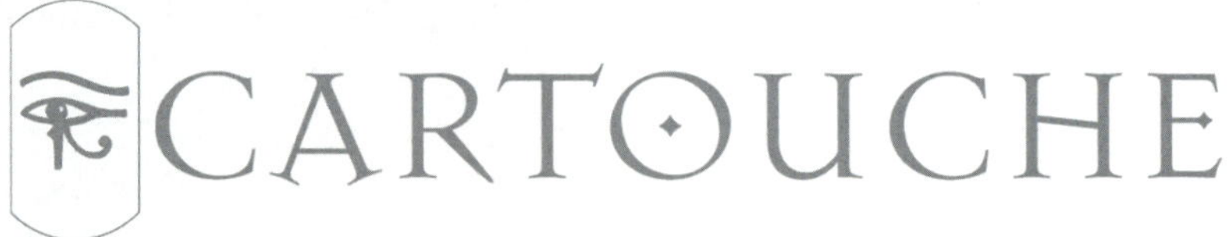

On the Cover: One of my personal favorites. I have about 10 pieces, in all of the work I have done, that stand as examples of where I would like to go. I like the texture, perhaps because of the way it seems to blend so well with the background. It would be hard for me to do something else like this and not revisit at least some aspect of its tone.

why i'm glad i'm a writer:
an appreciation of christopher shy

by Kenneth Hite

I used to draw. I used to draw a lot. My folks did a lot of volunteer work that involved massive reams of paper printed on one side – petition drives, letters to Congress, mailbox fliers, that sort of thing – and so there was always leftover paper to draw on. And on, and on. I drew houses, and superheroes, and all kinds of things that kids draw.

And I drew monsters.

I used to think I was pretty good at it, and I eventually even earned some occasional bucks or a little prestige drawing, but eventually I realized that drawing was very hard work, and so I became a writer instead, because as everyone knows, writing is the easiest thing in the world. I write about conspiracies, and magic, and Klingons, and zeppelins.

And I write about monsters.

I also write about roleplaying games, which are the sorts of things Christopher Shy tends to illustrate – and right there, that's reason enough to take up this hobby, in the hope that while you're buying roleplaying game books you'll be lucky enough to buy ones like ***All Flesh Must Be Eaten*** or ***Clanbook: Nosferatu*** or ***Obsidian*** or ***Conspiracy X*** or ***Infernalism: the Path of Screams*** or (ahem) ***GURPS Cabal***, and you'll get some Christopher Shy art to go along with them.

I've written a lot of words in my life, as it happens, for a lot of people. But I've begun to notice something. Whenever people whose job it is to know about artists read my writing, they all seem to say the same thing – "I like what you wrote about Christopher Shy's art." "Uhh, yeah," I say, "I wrote that he's great, and that he's superb, and that he just keeps getting better the longer he does it, and I wrote that he does creepy menace better than anyone who isn't Clive Barker, and I've even used big, exciting Latinate words like 'transcendent' and 'evocative'. Oh, and I also wrote ABOUT A HALF A MILLION WORDS THAT DON'T HAVE ANYTHING TO DO WITH CHRISTOPHER SHY." "Yeah, well, you were right about Christopher Shy's art."

This, for those of you who were wondering, is why I'm glad I became a writer – for the respect.

No, I'm lying. I'm glad I became a writer, because if I'd stayed with my early precocious art talent, and gone to art school, and worked very very hard at it, and learned all that stuff about muscle shapes and chiaroscuro and false perspective, and slowly perfected my craft until it truly shone and glistened with creative blood – well, if I'd done that, I'd have to quit now, because Christopher Shy probably makes better art pouring gravy on biscuits than I'd make after thirty years at the feet of Caravaggio.

Who, since I'm a writer, I'm allowed to know about, and if you won't take it as a little too precious for words, I'd like to mention that although an artist would probably say that they haven't got much in common, as a writer they both give me the living creeps.

Because they both paint monsters.

Even, or perhaps even especially, when they're not. No, no, that's just St. Jerome, they say, or a guy in an alley with a very informal clothing sense. But you and I know that they're really monsters.

Now, lots of people say they paint monsters, and sometimes, sure, they do. H.R. Giger, in between plumbing schematics and pus-covered insect heads, has probably painted two or maybe three monsters. I'm sure if you sifted through every single canvas by every single "horror" artist alive, you'd run across nine, maybe ten or twelve, monsters.

But I'll let you in on it – all of Christopher Shy's stuff is about monsters. Because frankly, whether you're a writer or an artist, or anyone else who spends any quality time in your own head – you know there's monsters there. And when you see them looking back at you from the page, well – it can give you the living creeps. Especially when you have to write about them. Because if I didn't write about them – I sure as hell couldn't draw them.

And then they couldn't get out.

And that's why I'm glad I'm a writer.

Kenneth Hite
Chicago, 2001

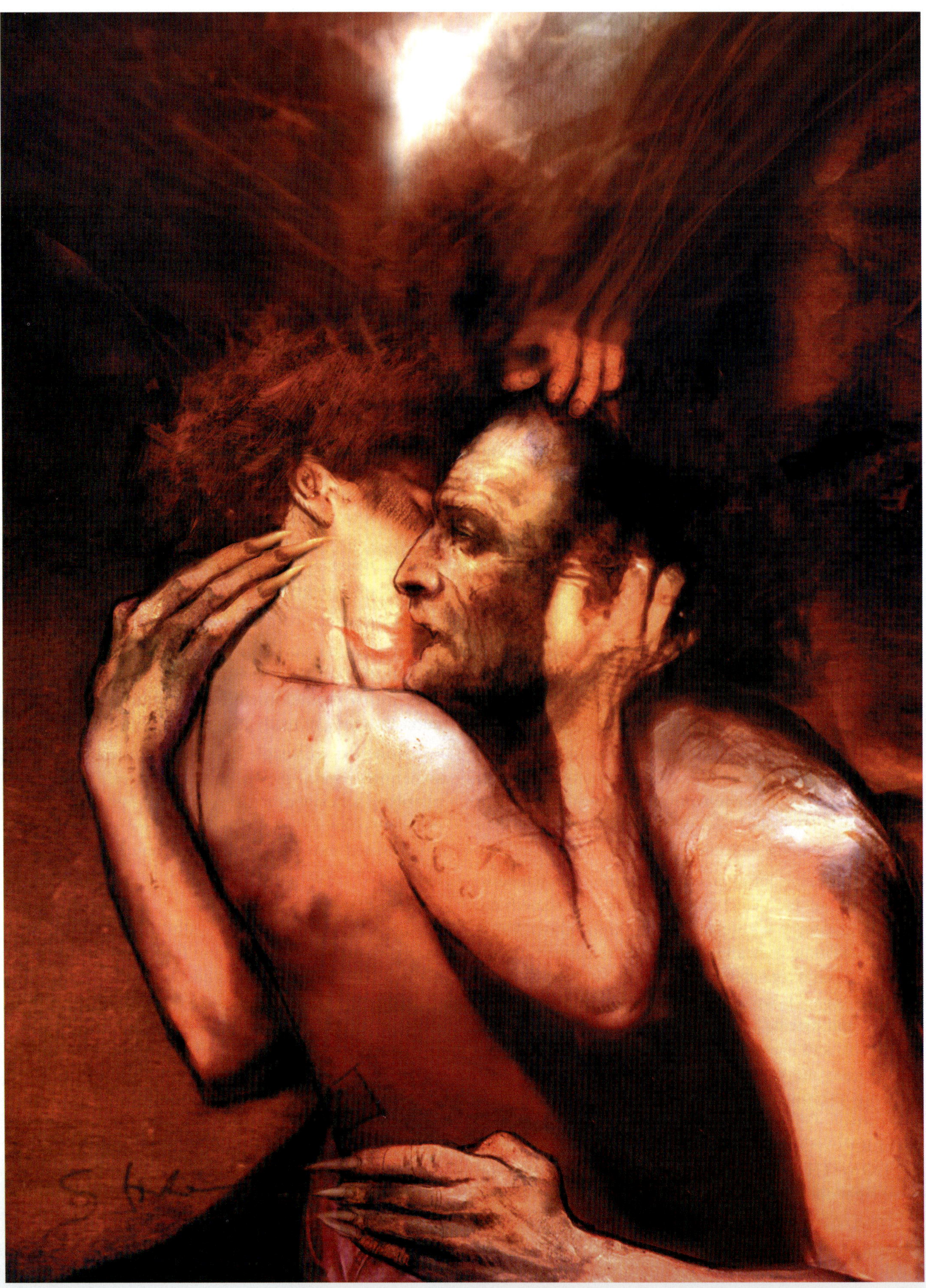

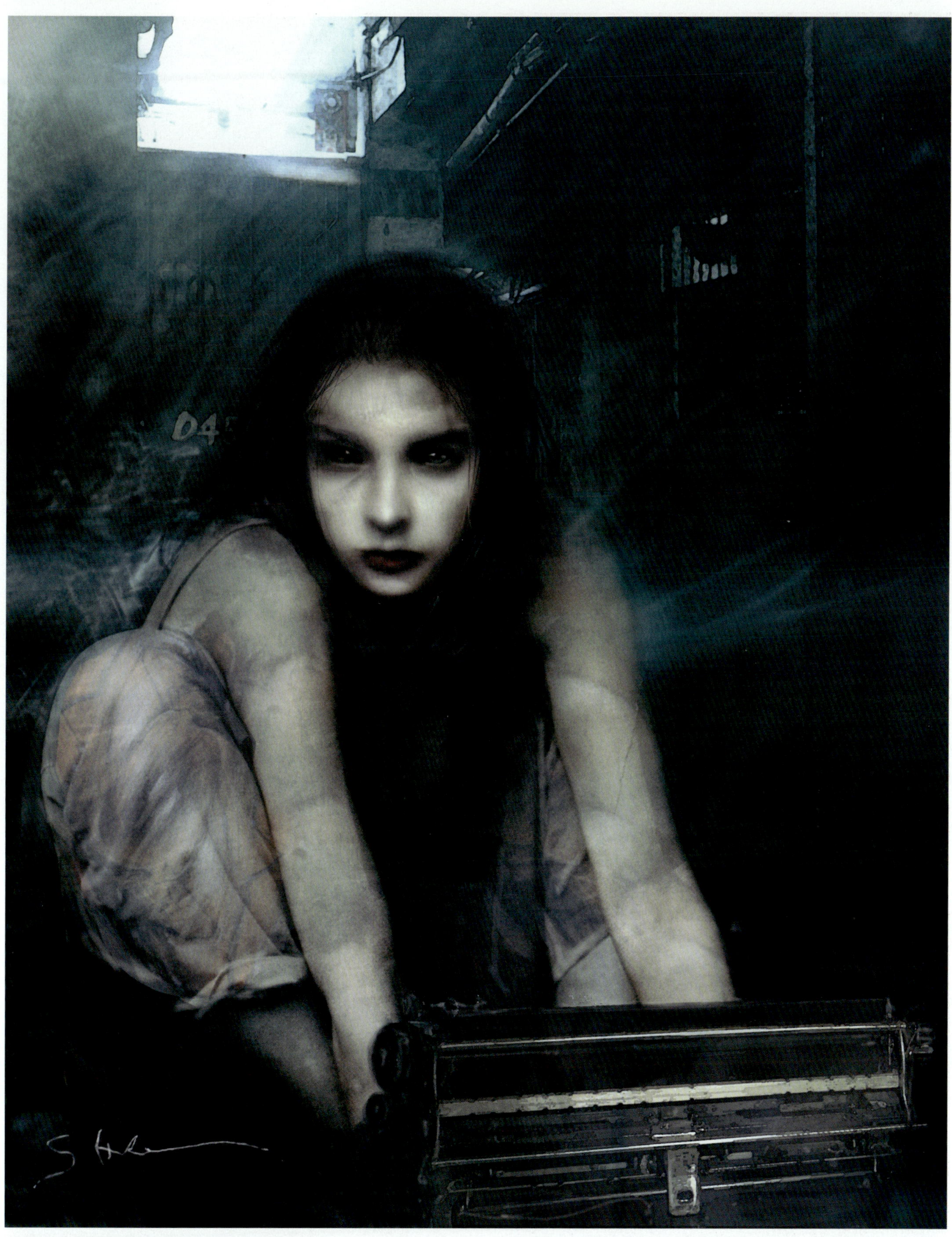

This one has a special meaning for me. I remember seeing this girl, a poet and writer, working one night, and thinking how relaxed she looked. Immersed in her writing, she seemed to curl like a cat at the machine. I loved the way she sat there, and tried to remember it as closely as I could.

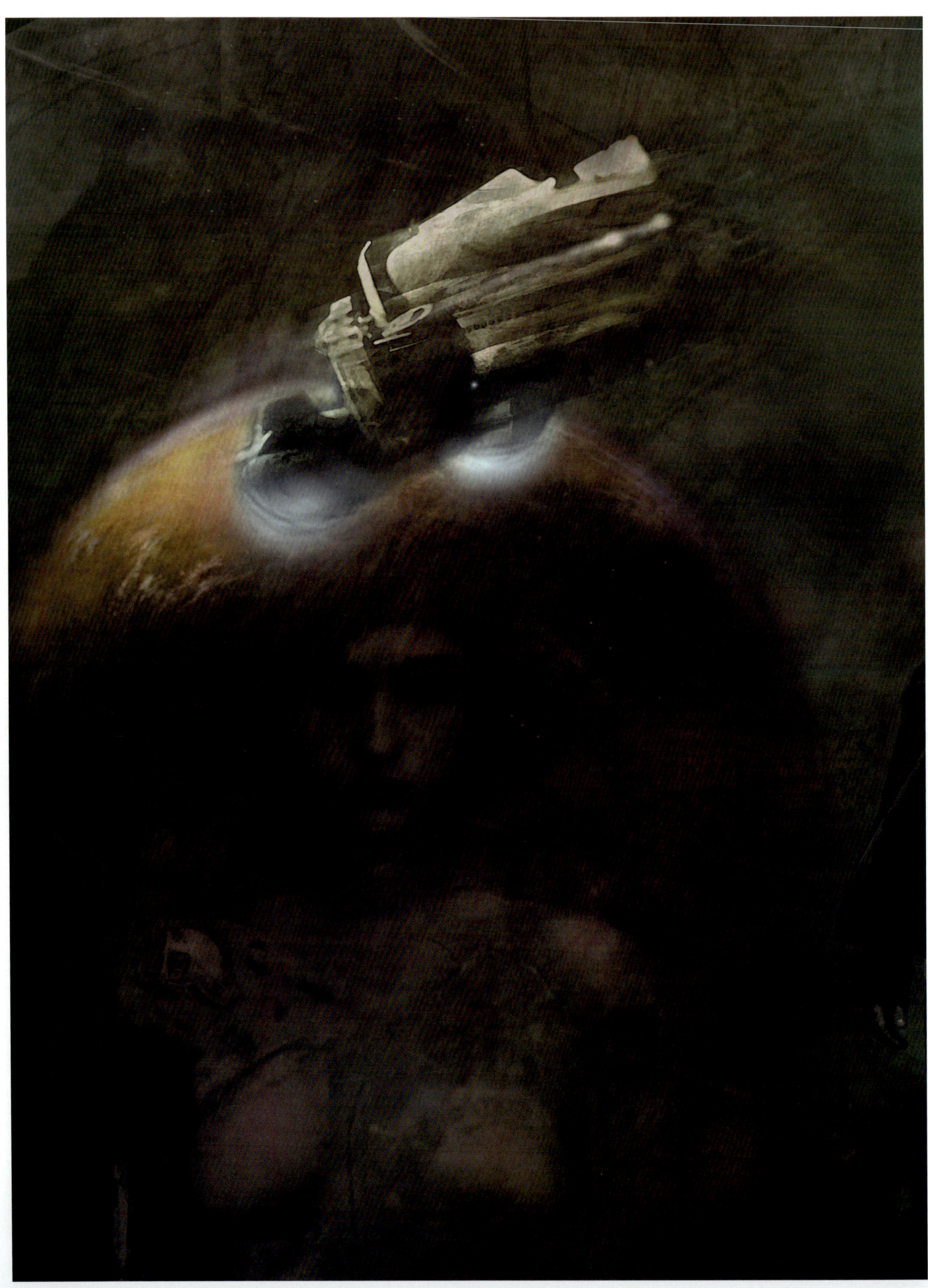

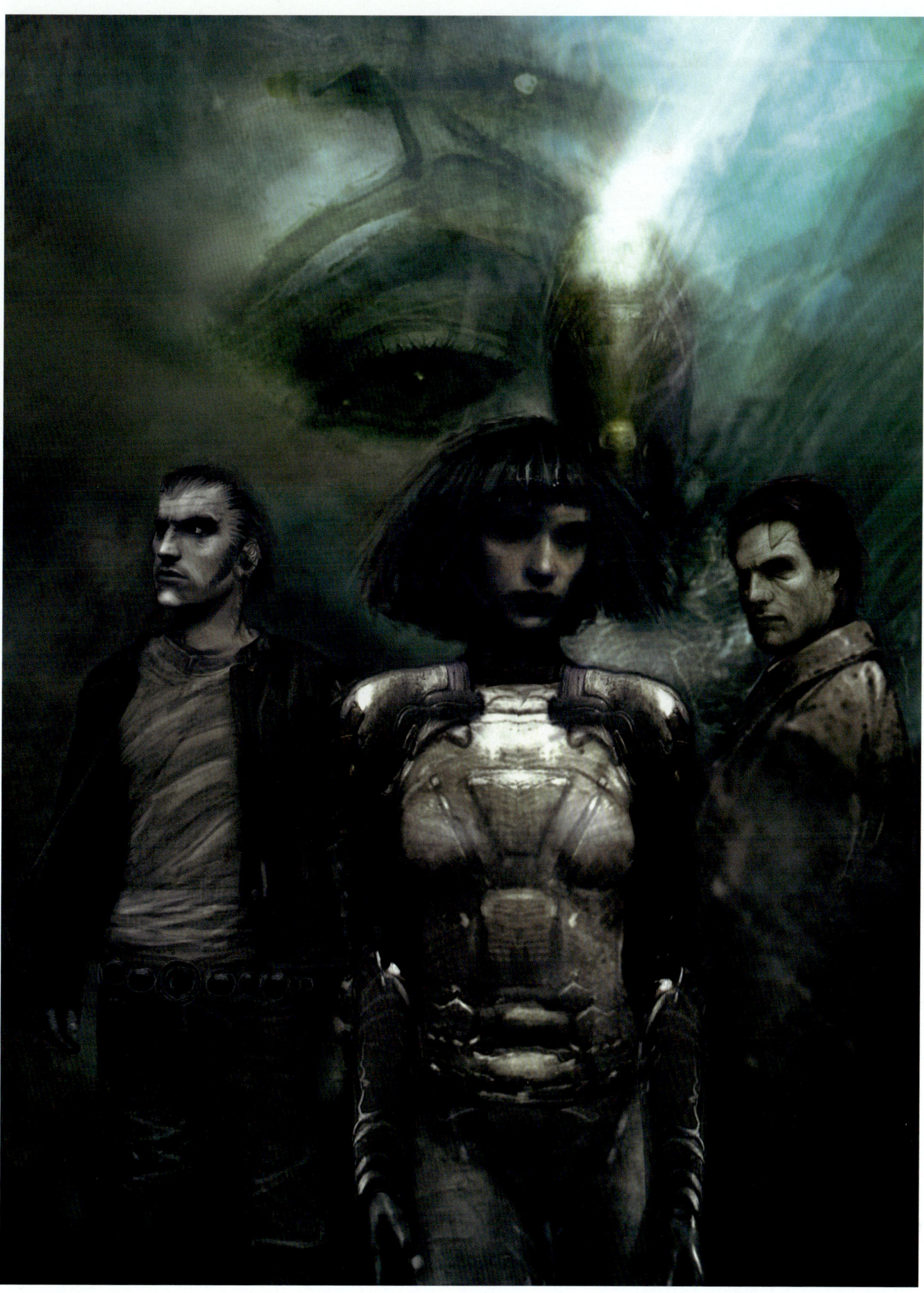

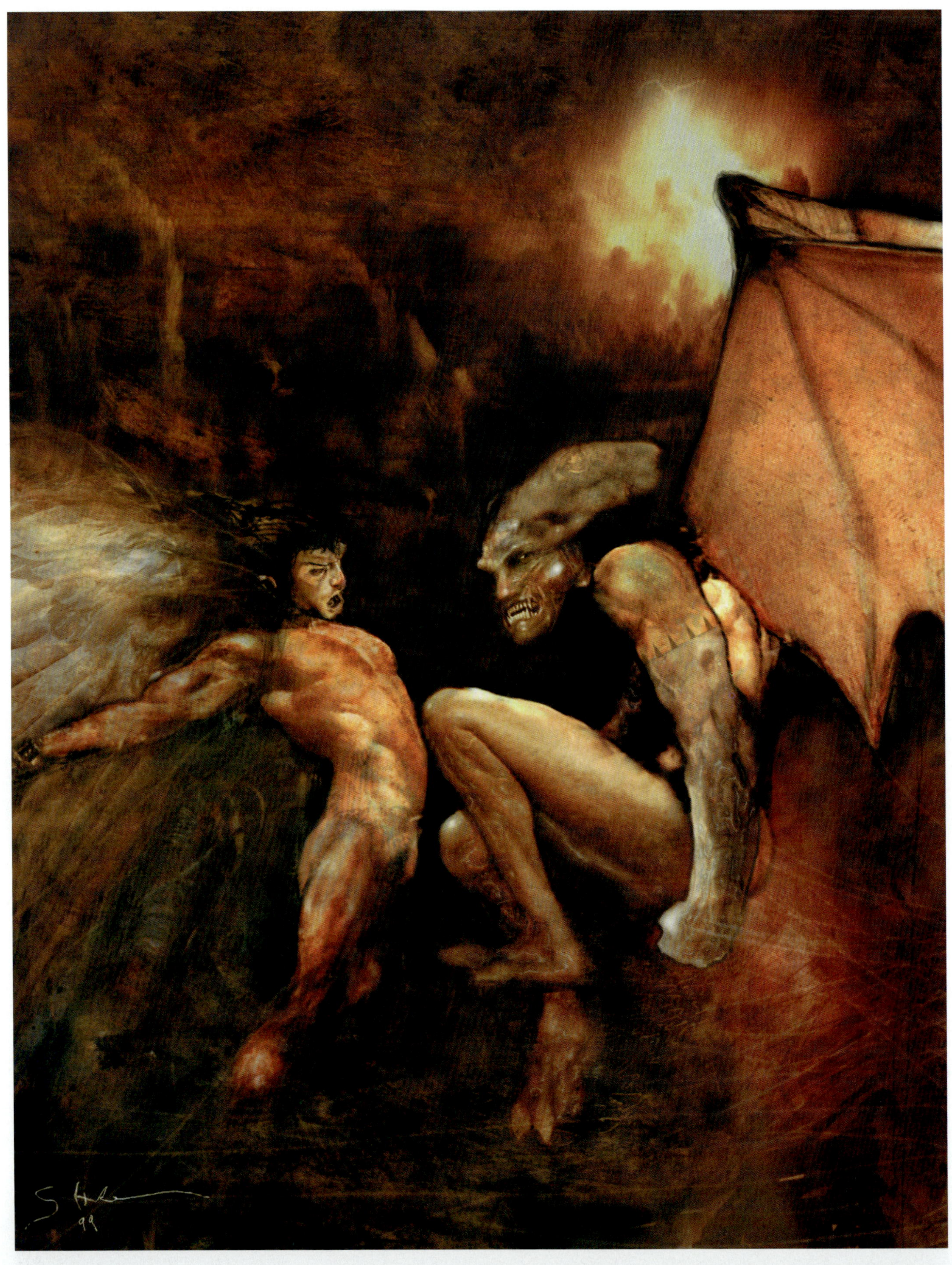

This painting was completed in 1999 for Steve Jackson Games' *GURPS In Nomine* game. It was rejected.

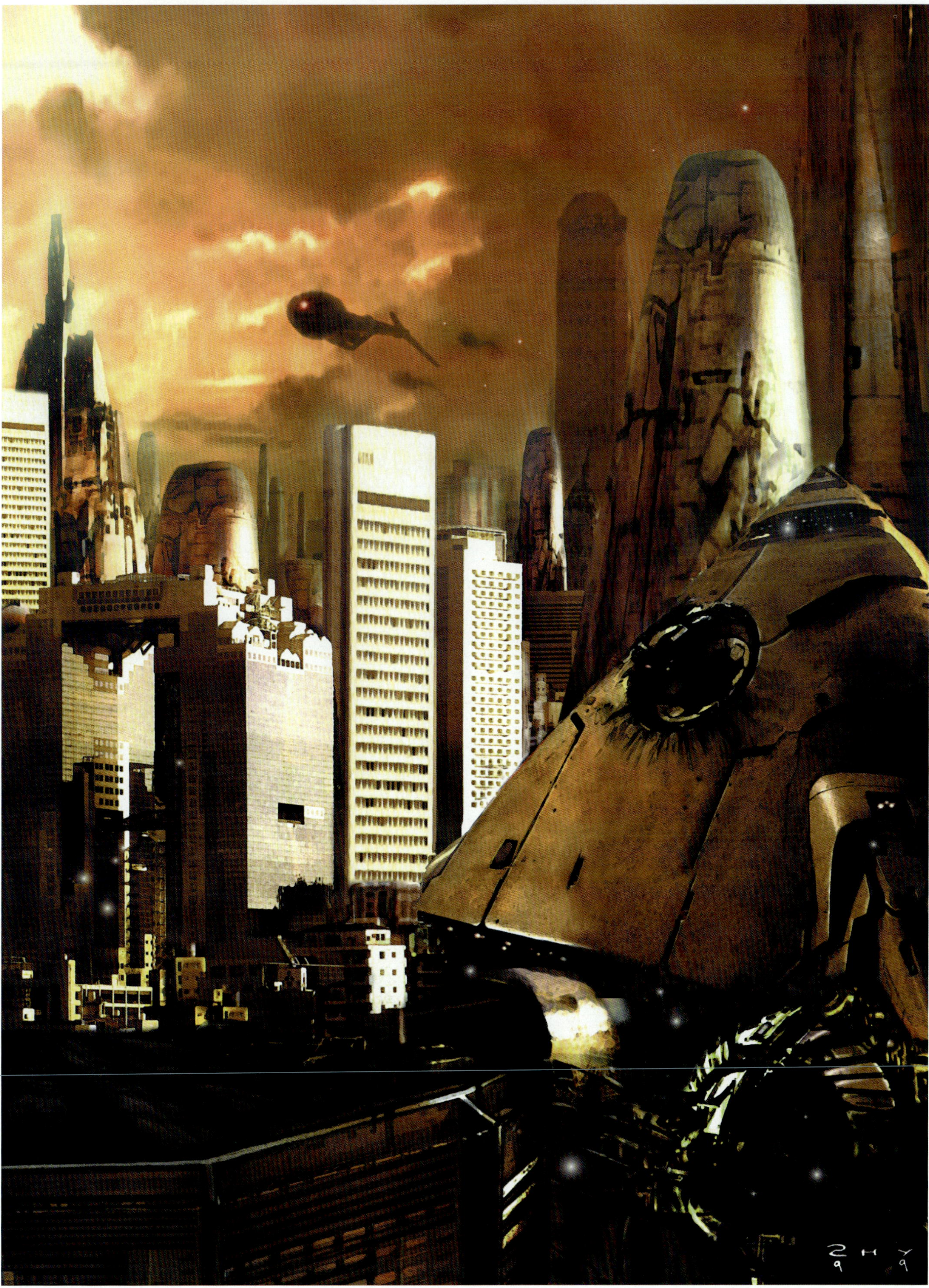

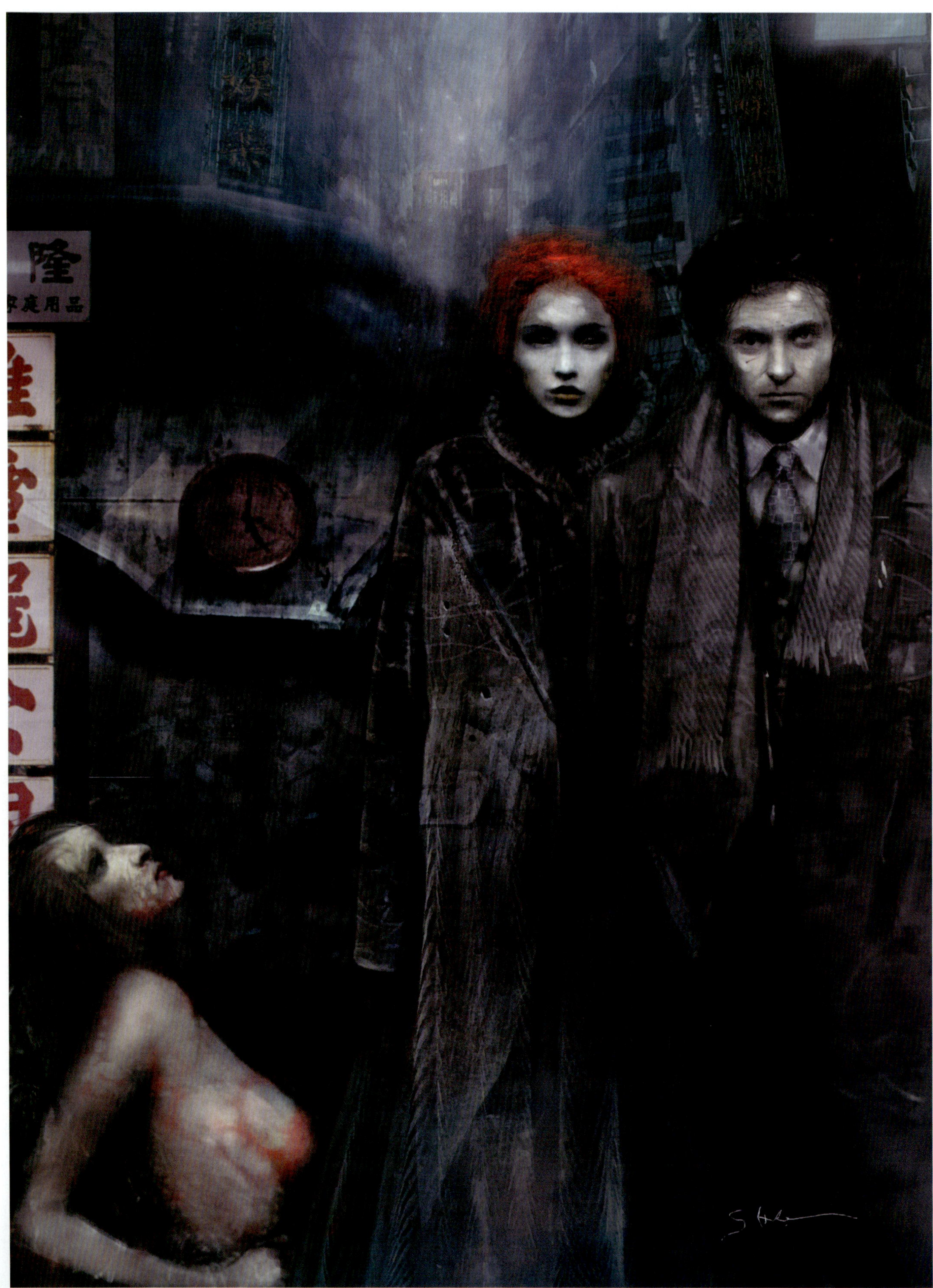

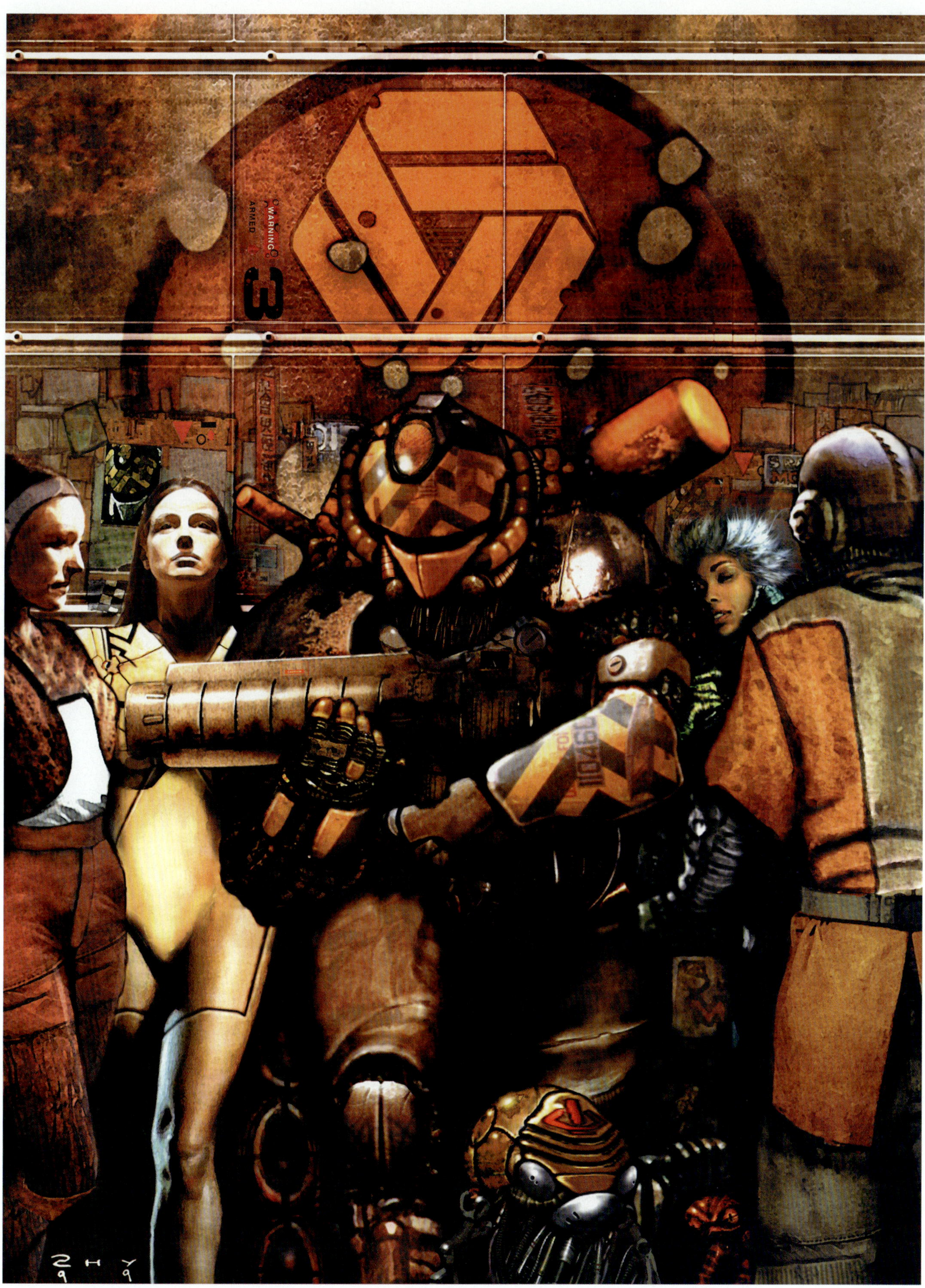

WARNING
ARMED
3

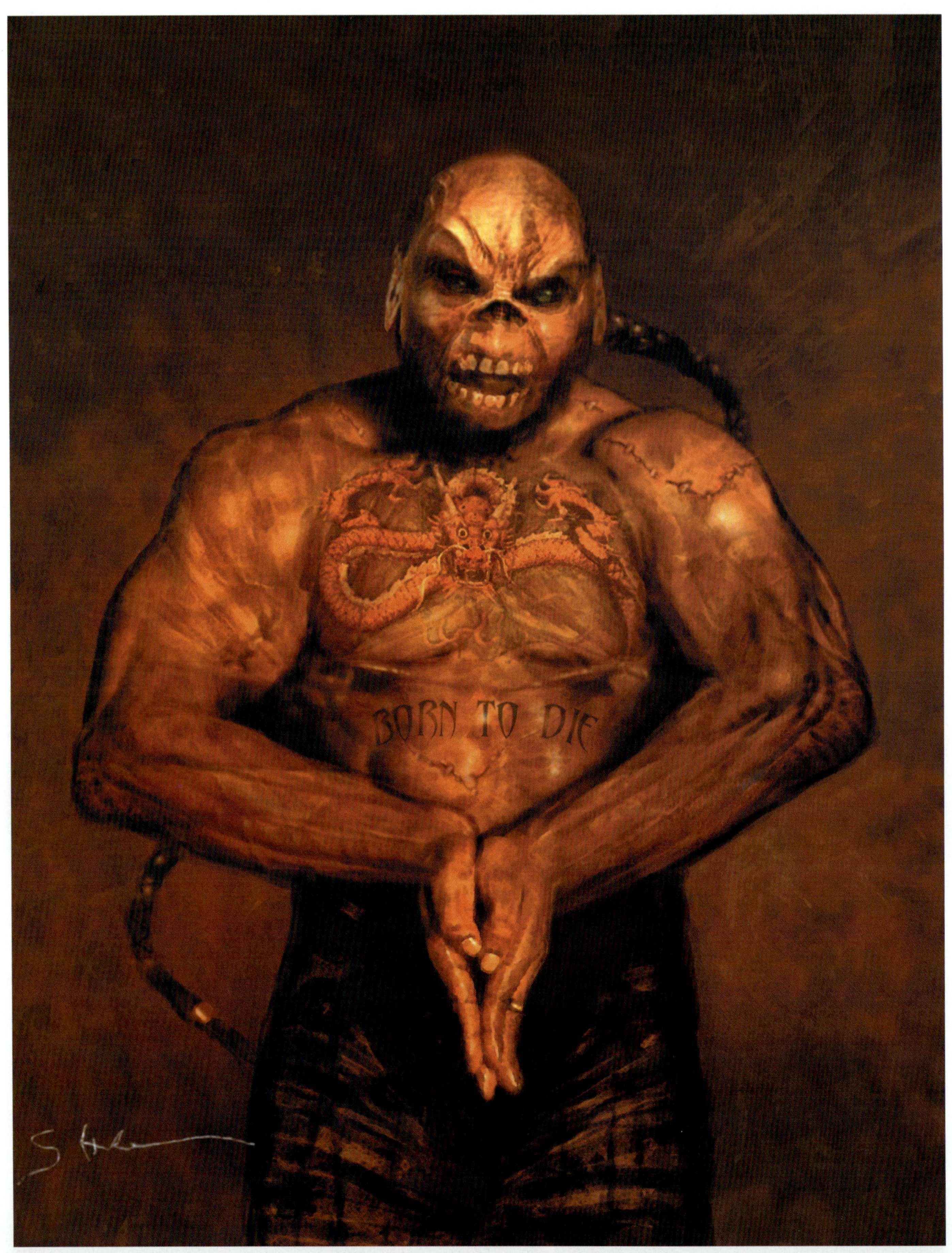

DeadBoy from *All Flesh Must Be Eaten*.
Who knew a game about zombies would become so popular? We did. In yer face.

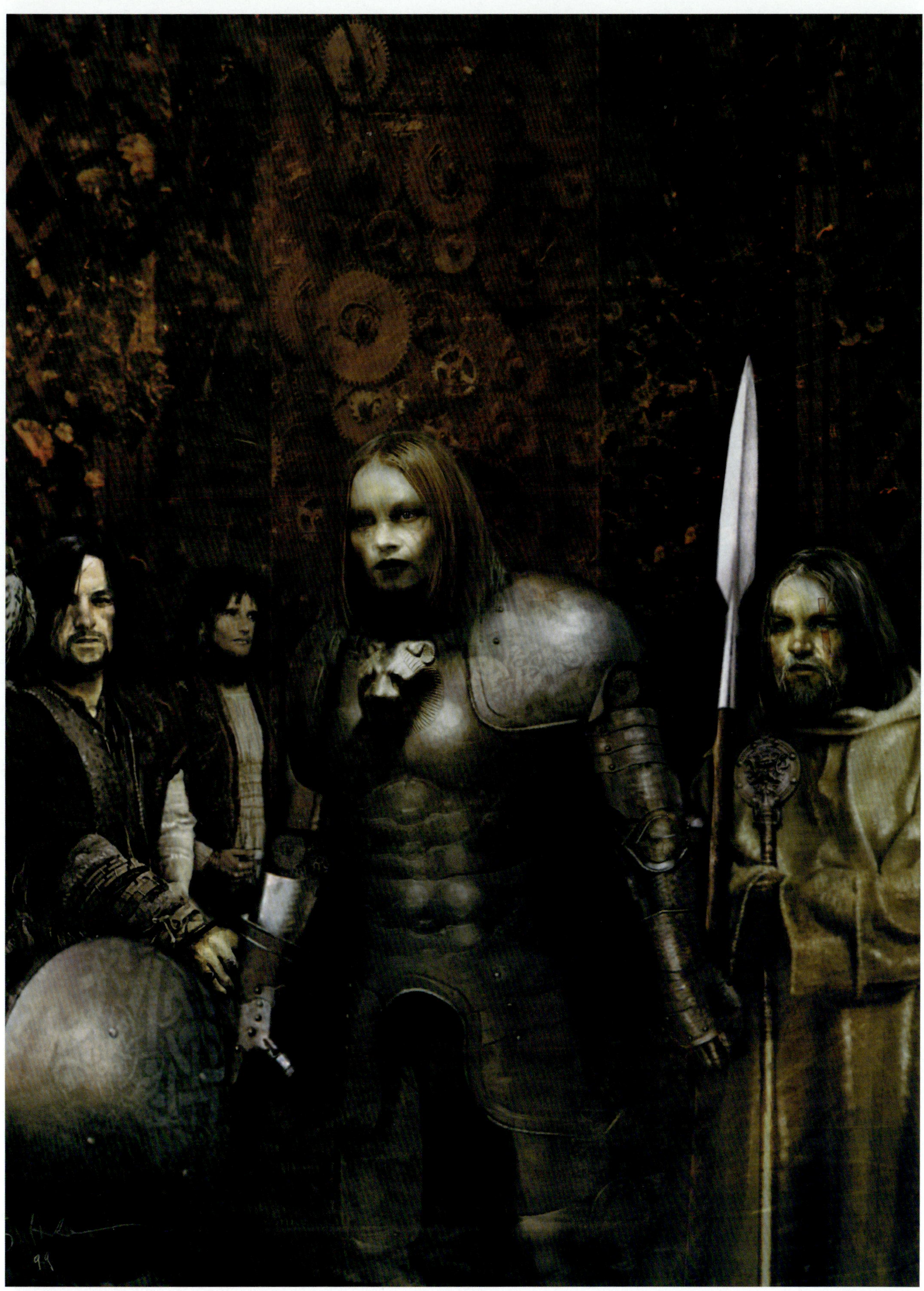

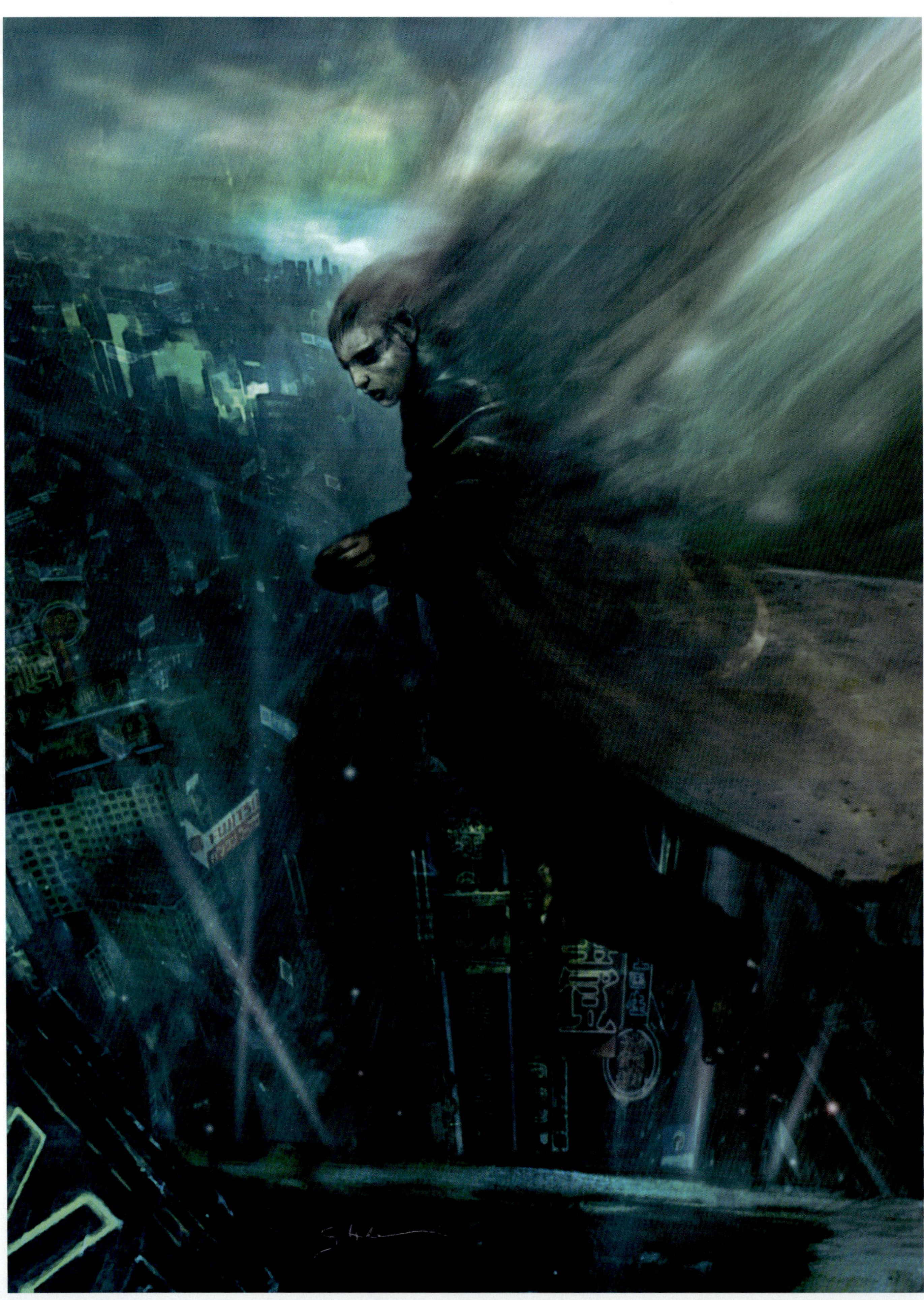

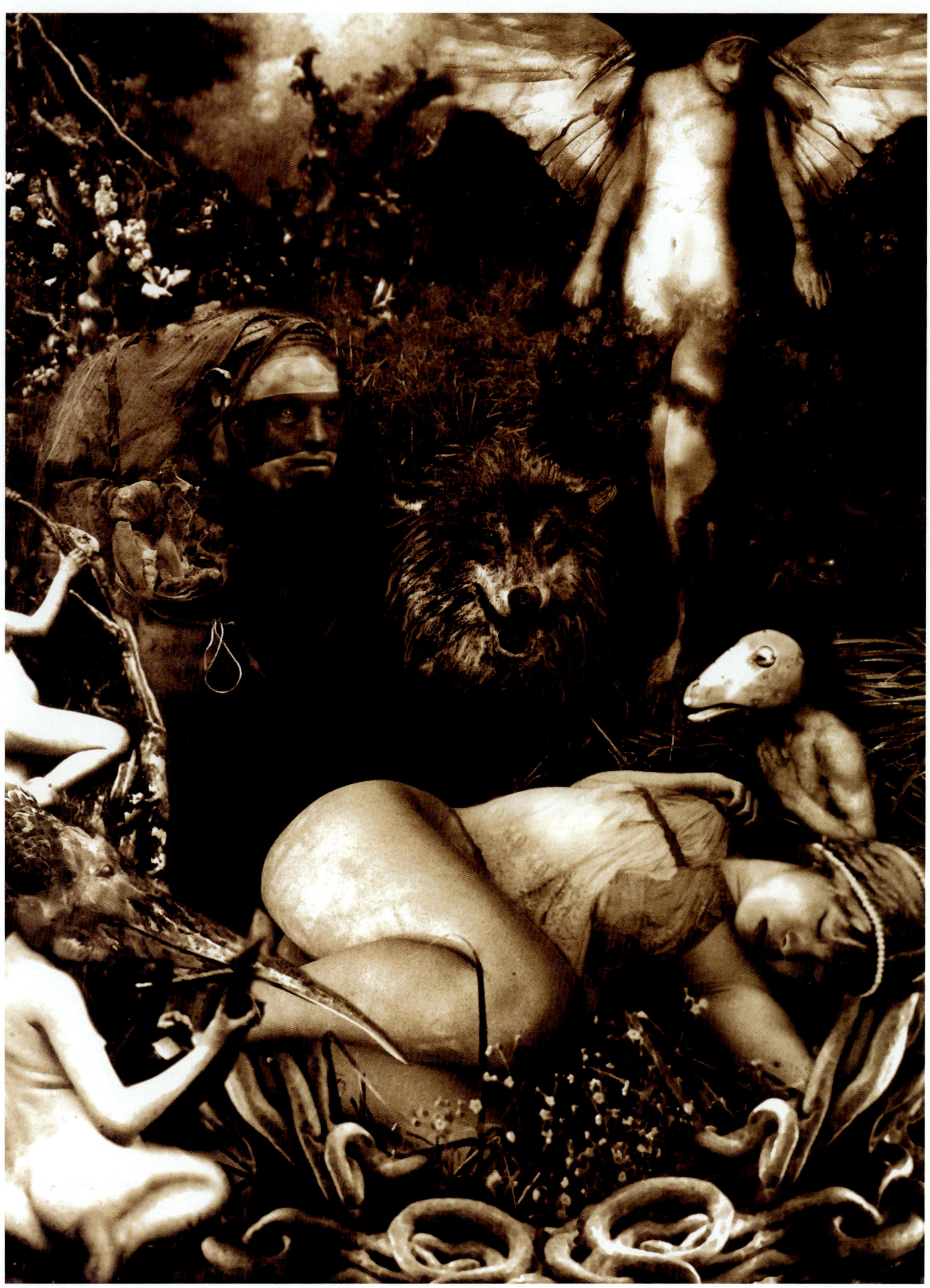

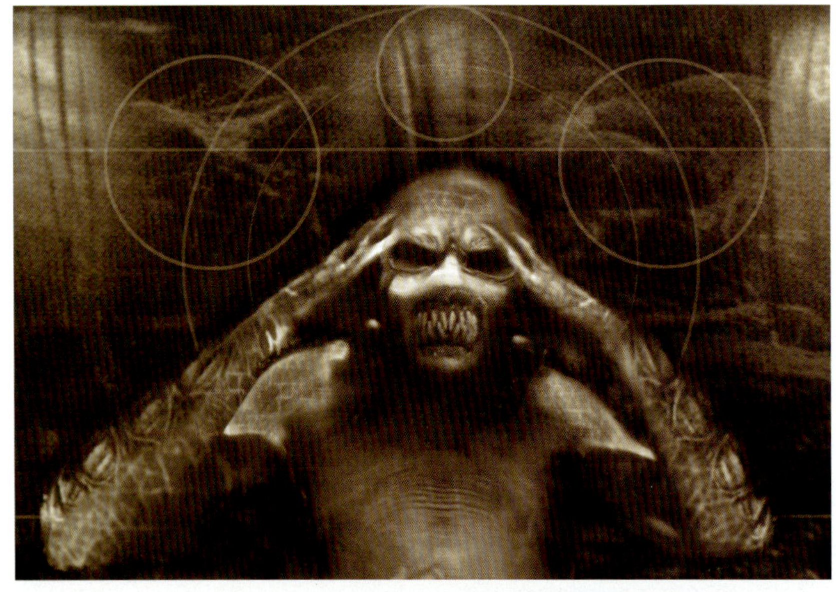

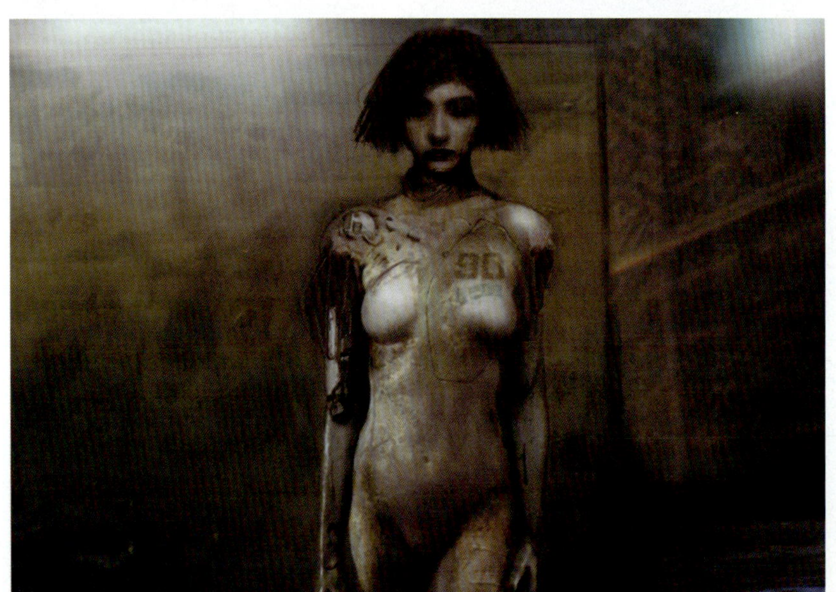

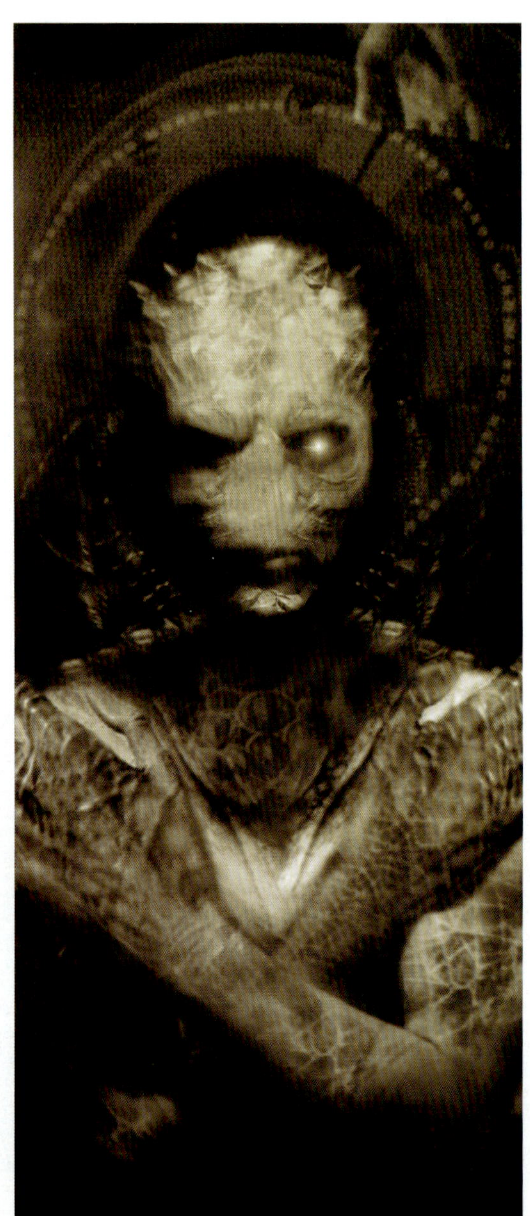

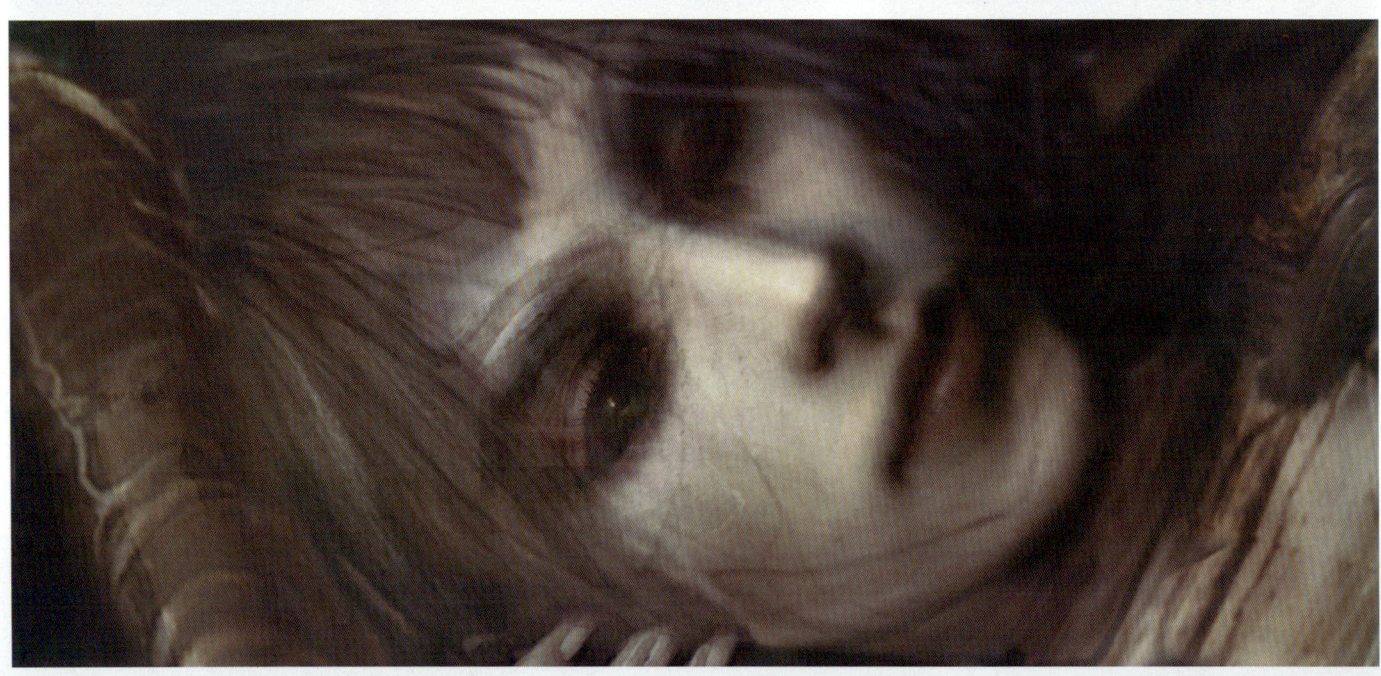

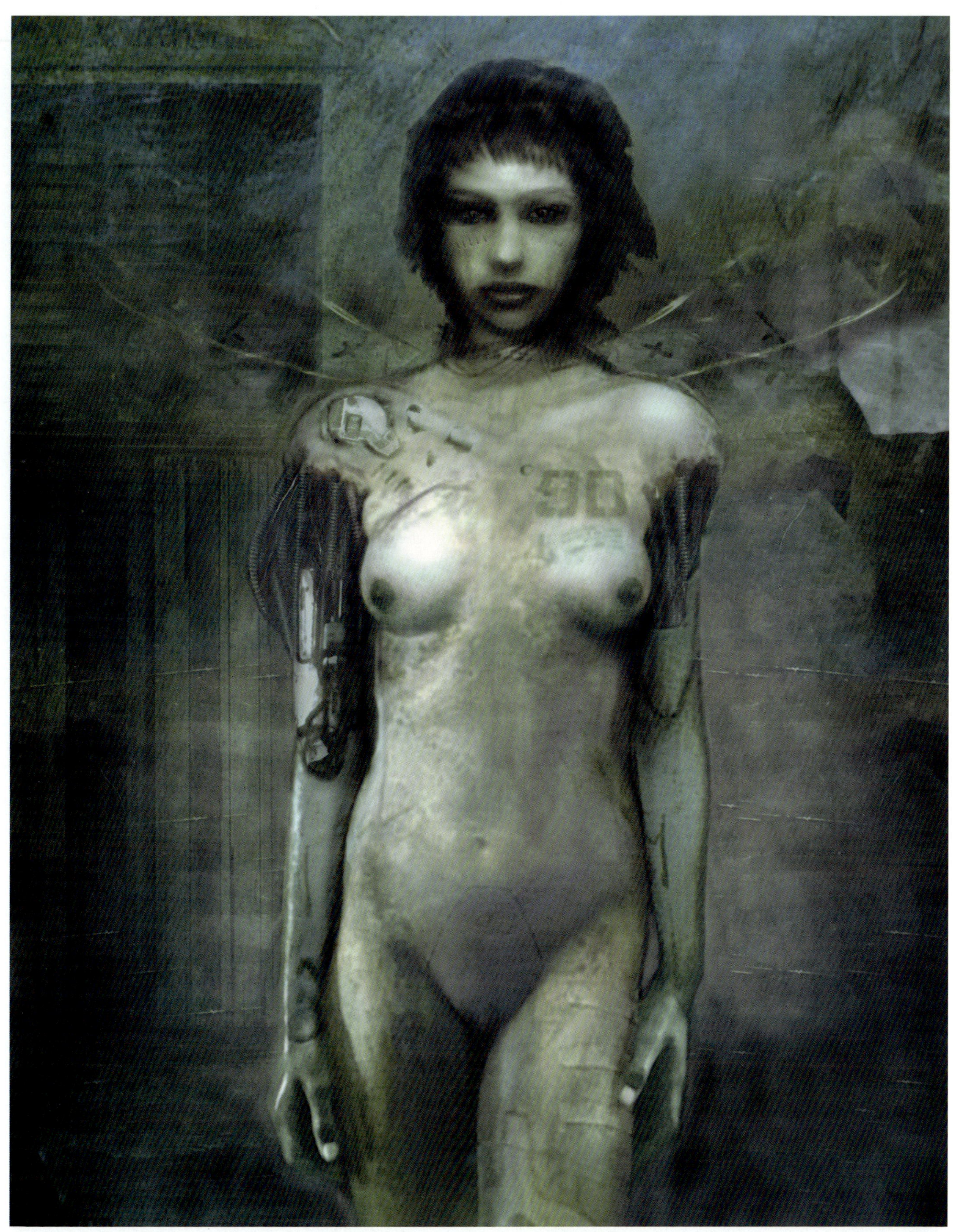

Close-up of Nadia from "Syndicate." The texture came from a half-dozen sources, laid down one at a time. It was this "Dead Flesh" look that would inspire Astropolitan Pictures to make a series of music videos later that year. It soon became a signature of a lot of my work.

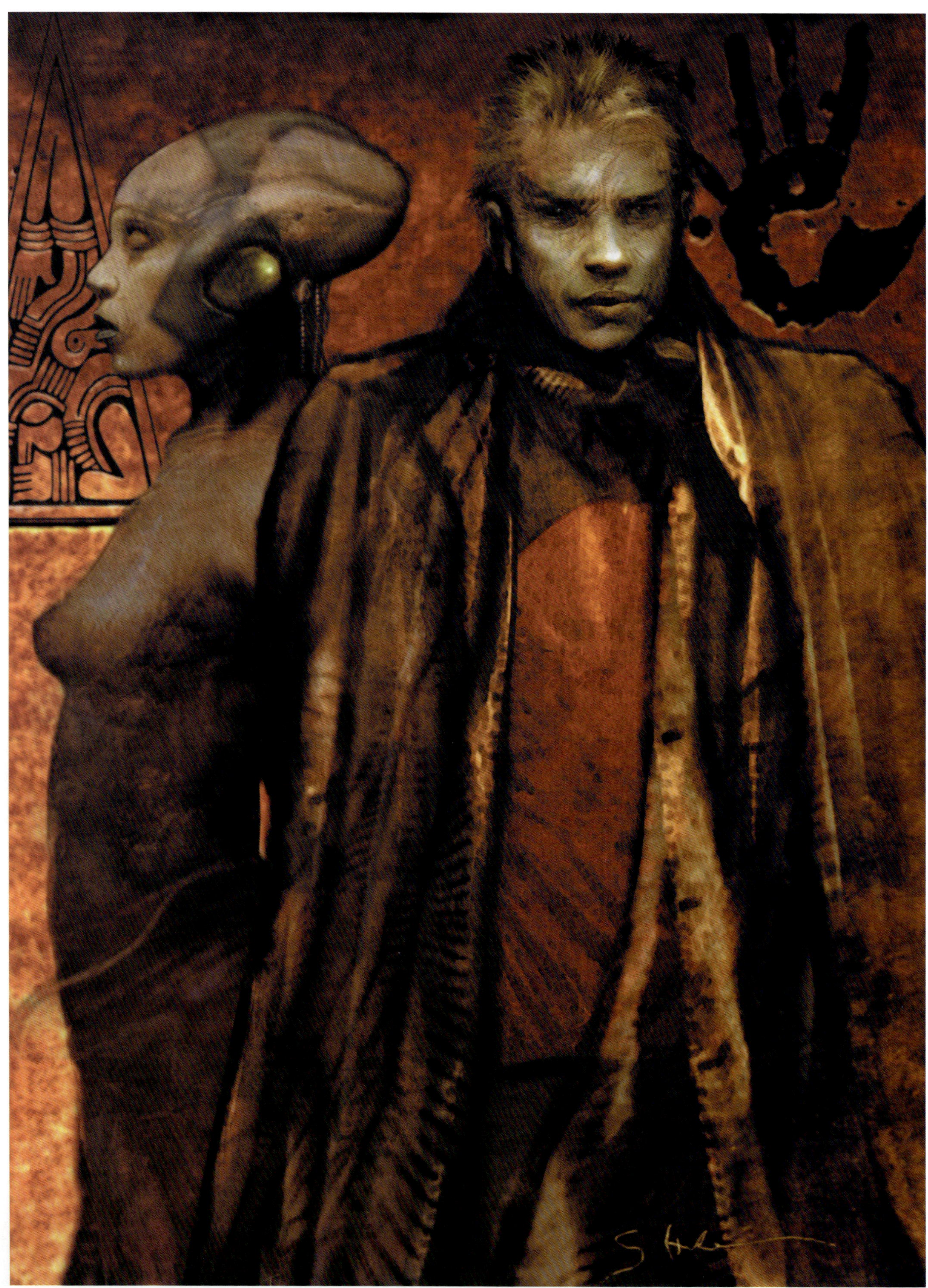

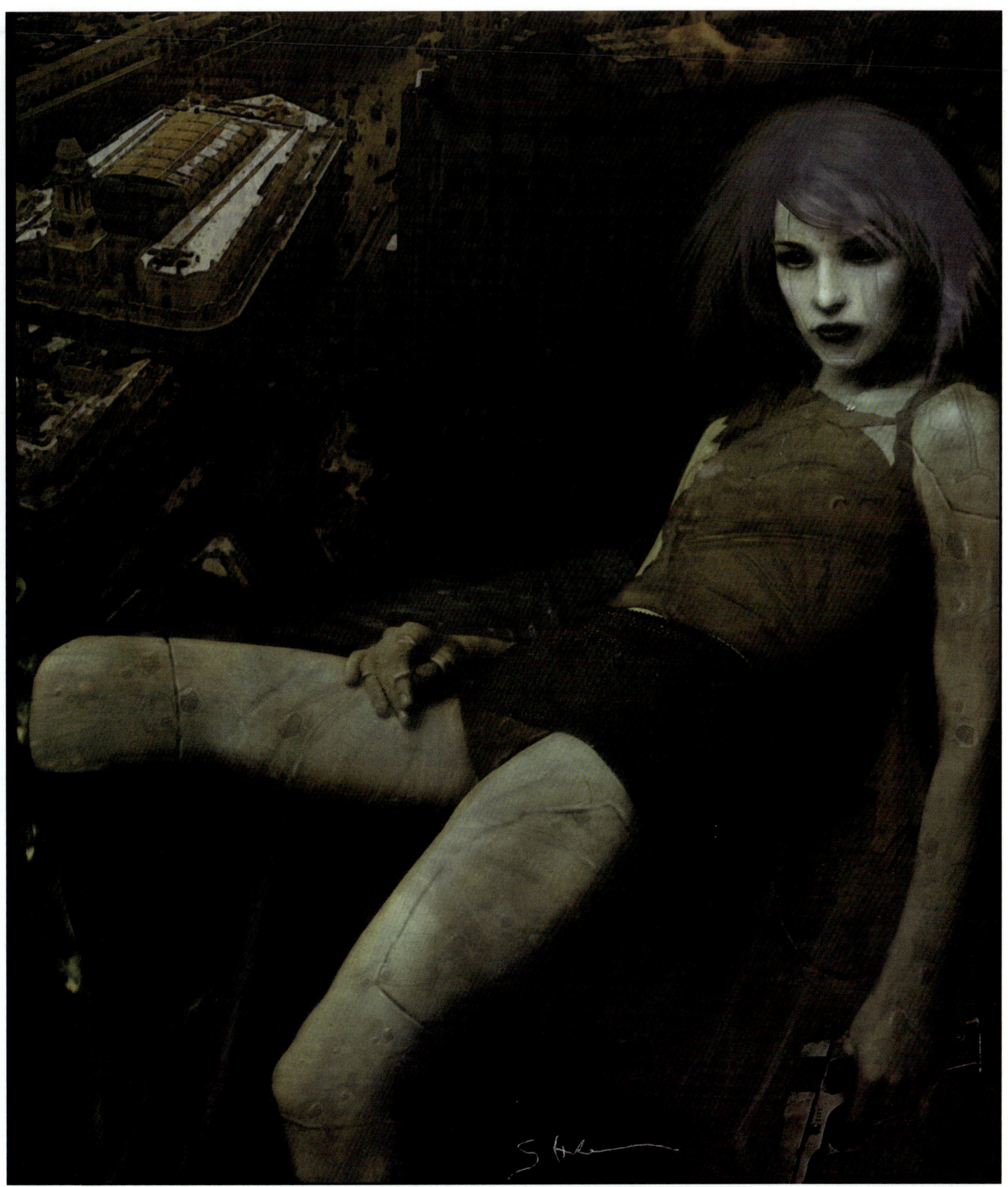

Philip Reed is one of my best friends. He is one of my art directors. He is also one of the rudest, meanest people I have ever met. If I were Hunter S. Thompson, he would have been my lawyer, feeding me drugs and publishing my books. I once watched him cut into four lanes of traffic, going through them horizontally while they were vertical, and screaming at them because they were in his way. He makes my life a living hell, and feeds me just enough money for my son and me to avoid starving. He butchers my work and kicks my cats. He steals from me and makes me do things against my will. Everything you ever heard about me is his fault. Make no mistake, Phil is an ass. Now look at this picture.

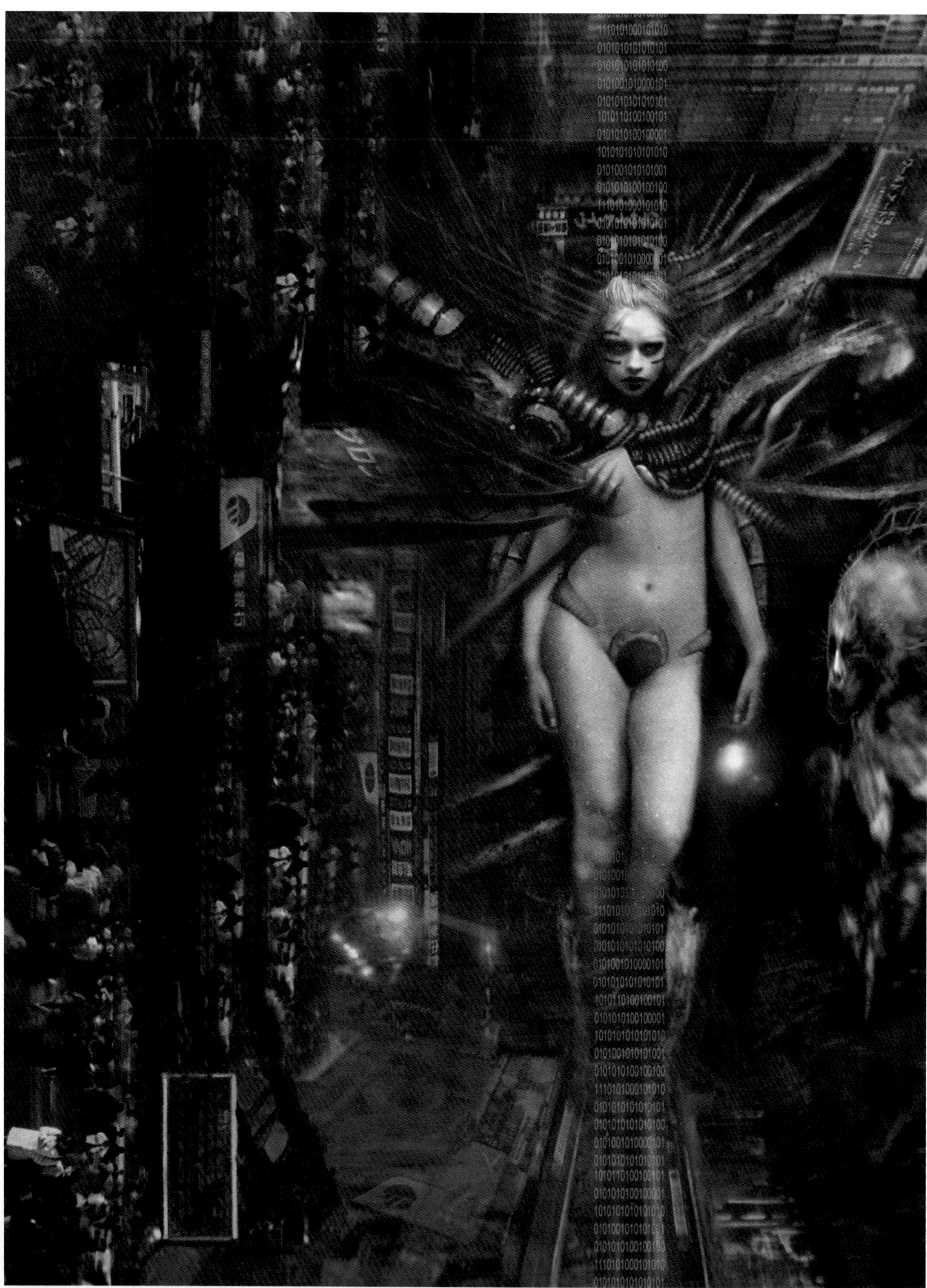

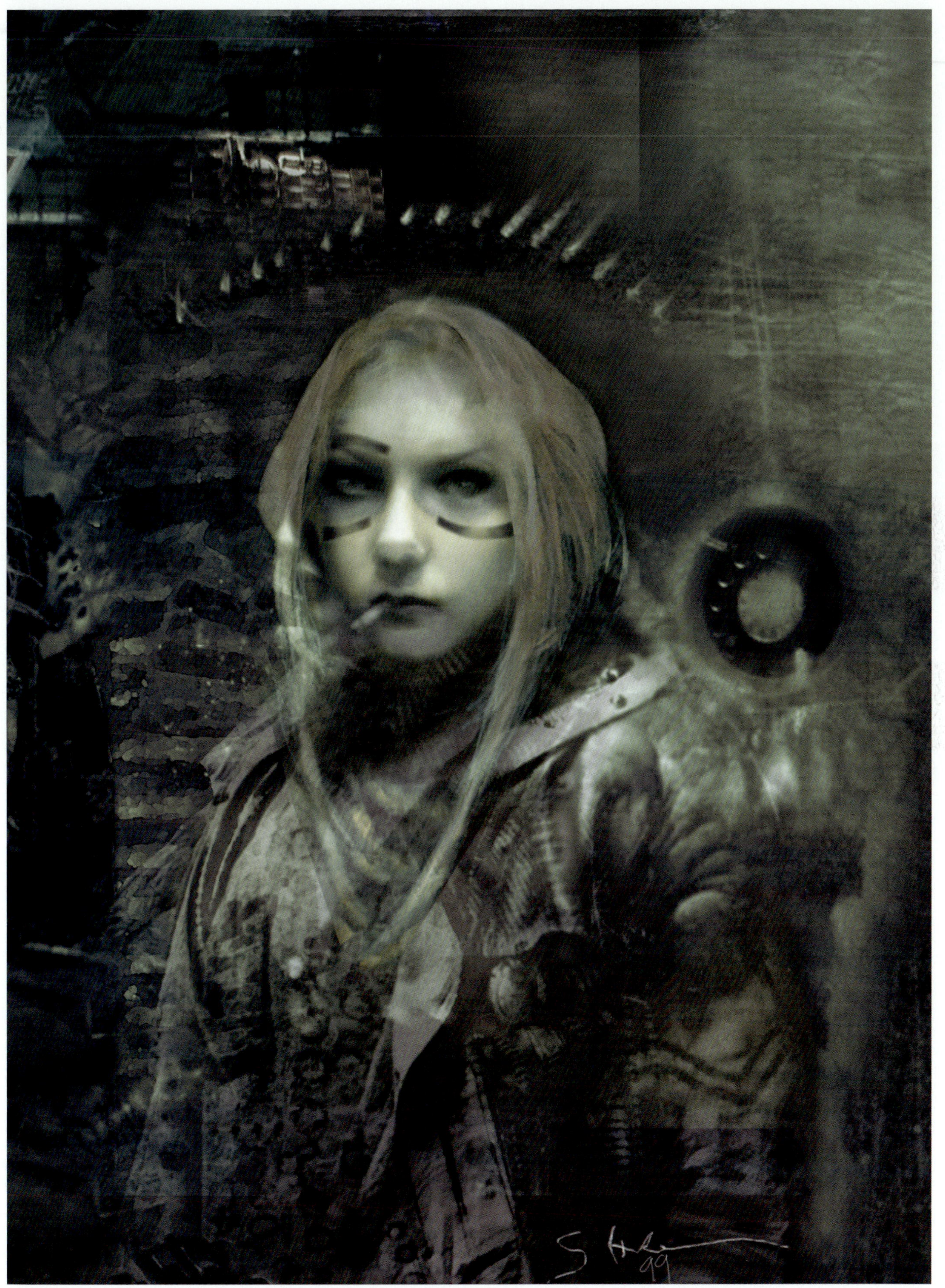

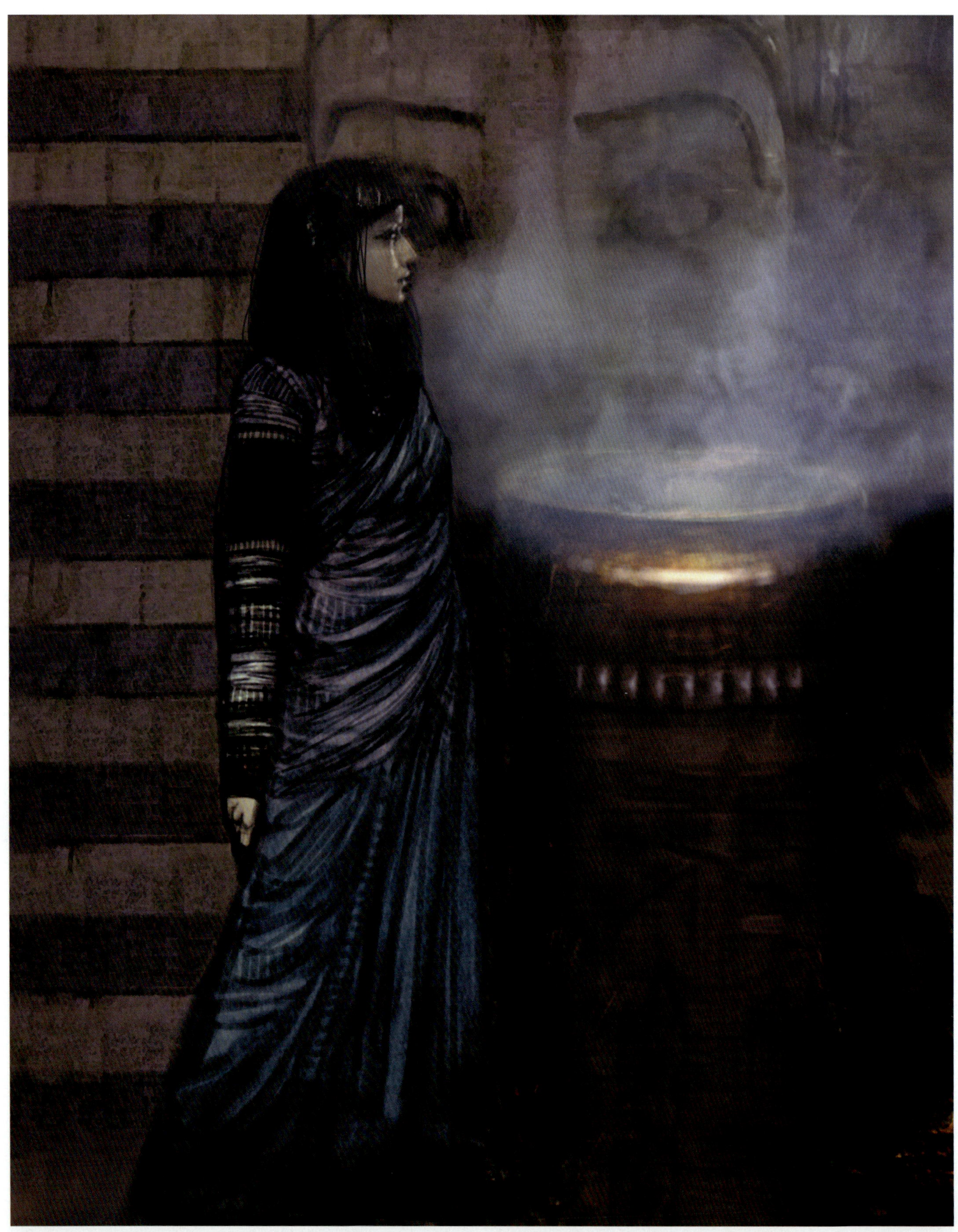

The great Flapper Debate. Who can do this hair better: Daniel or Christopher? Does it even really matter? Kati would disagree, to the point of dumping water on my lap when she discovered that Daniel had started to draw it on his figures as well. Jealously can be a very ugly thing. Thanks a lot, Kati.

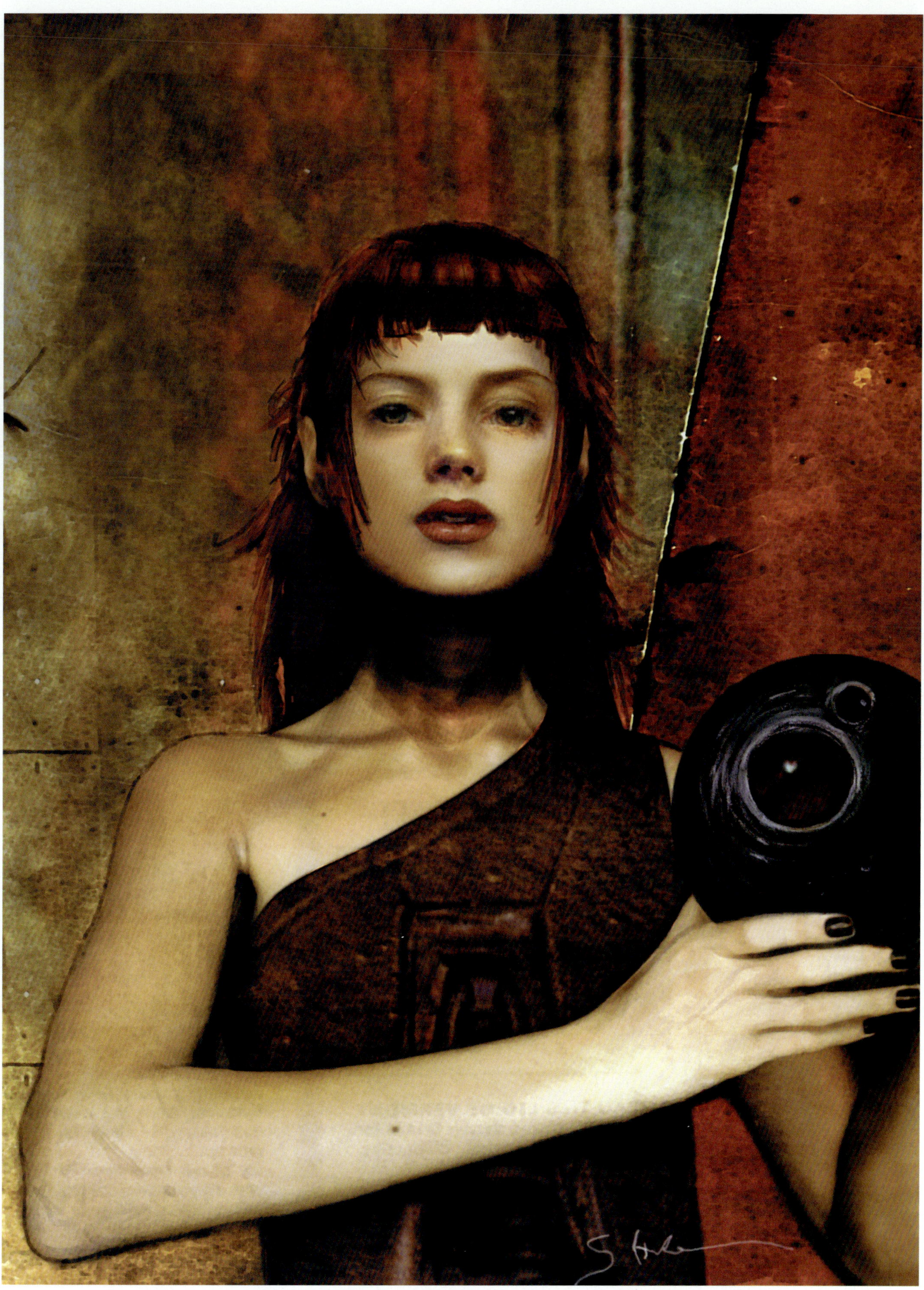

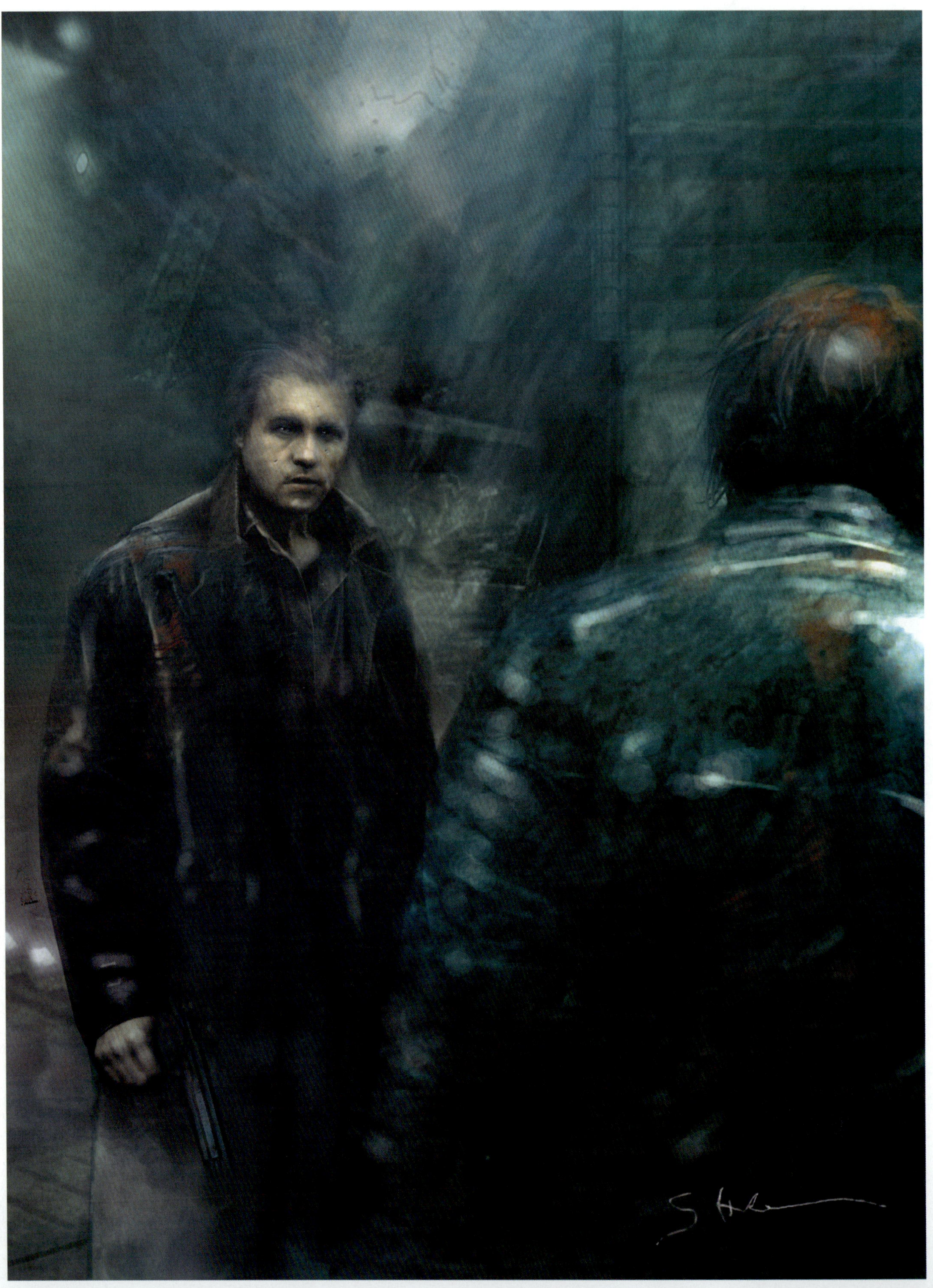

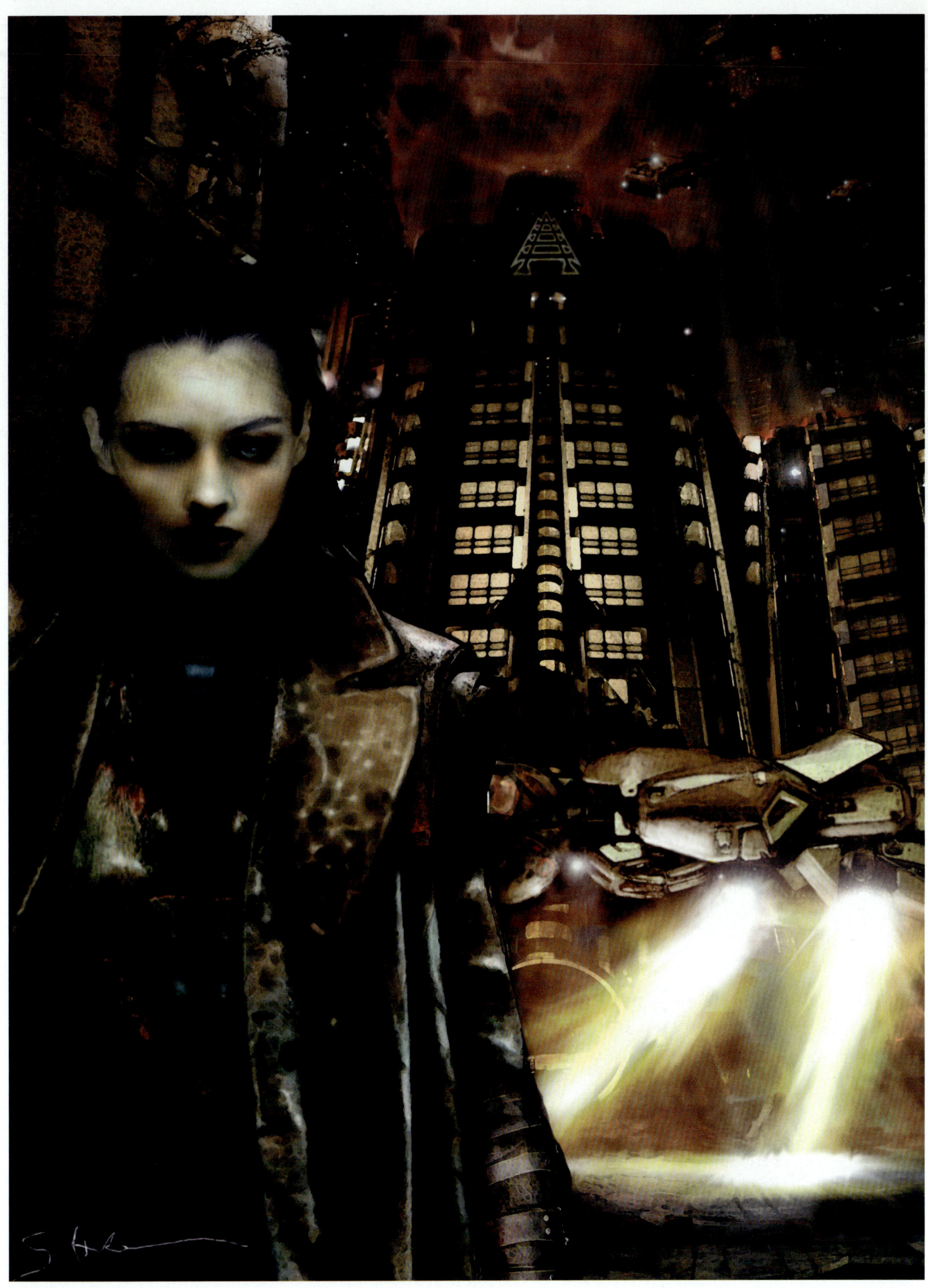

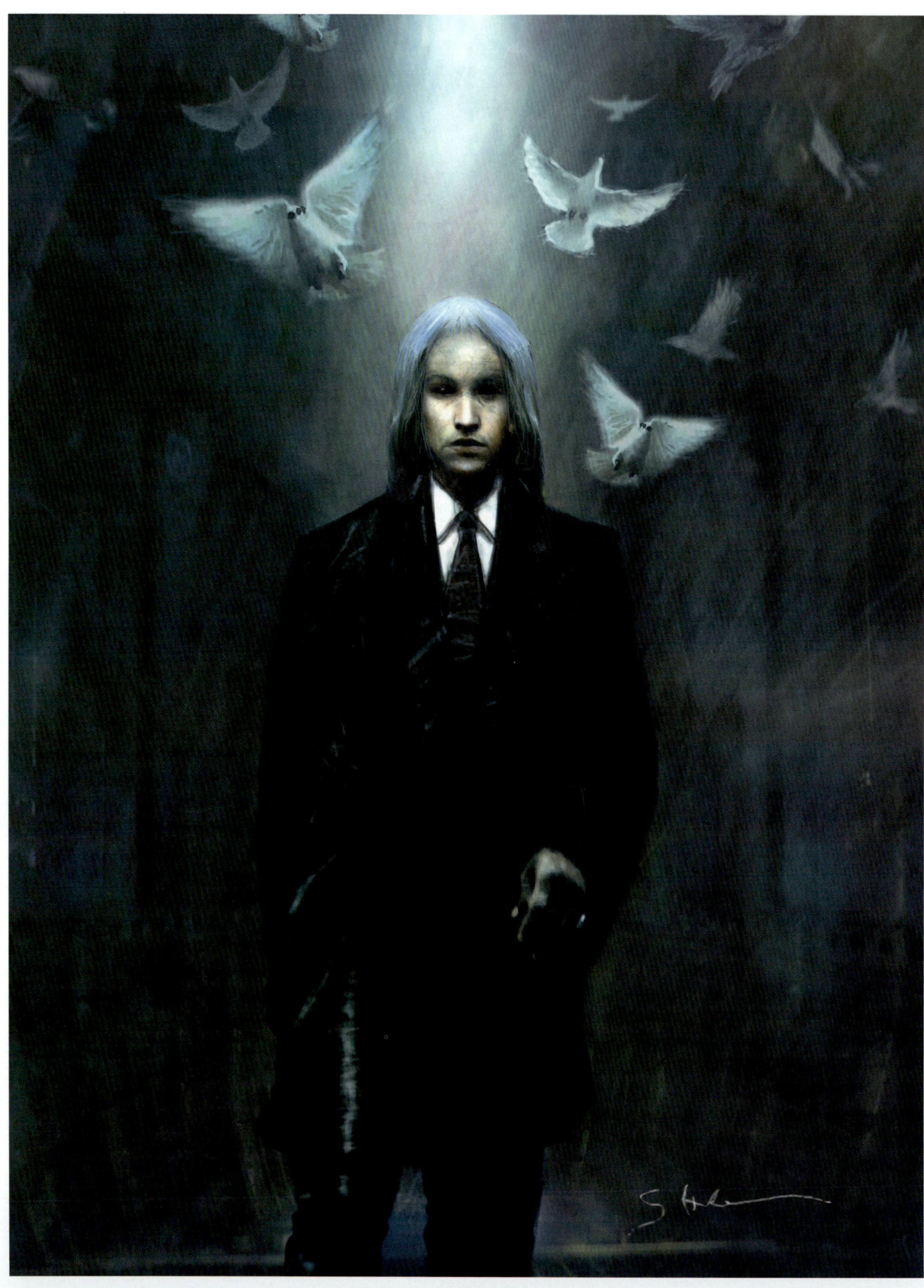

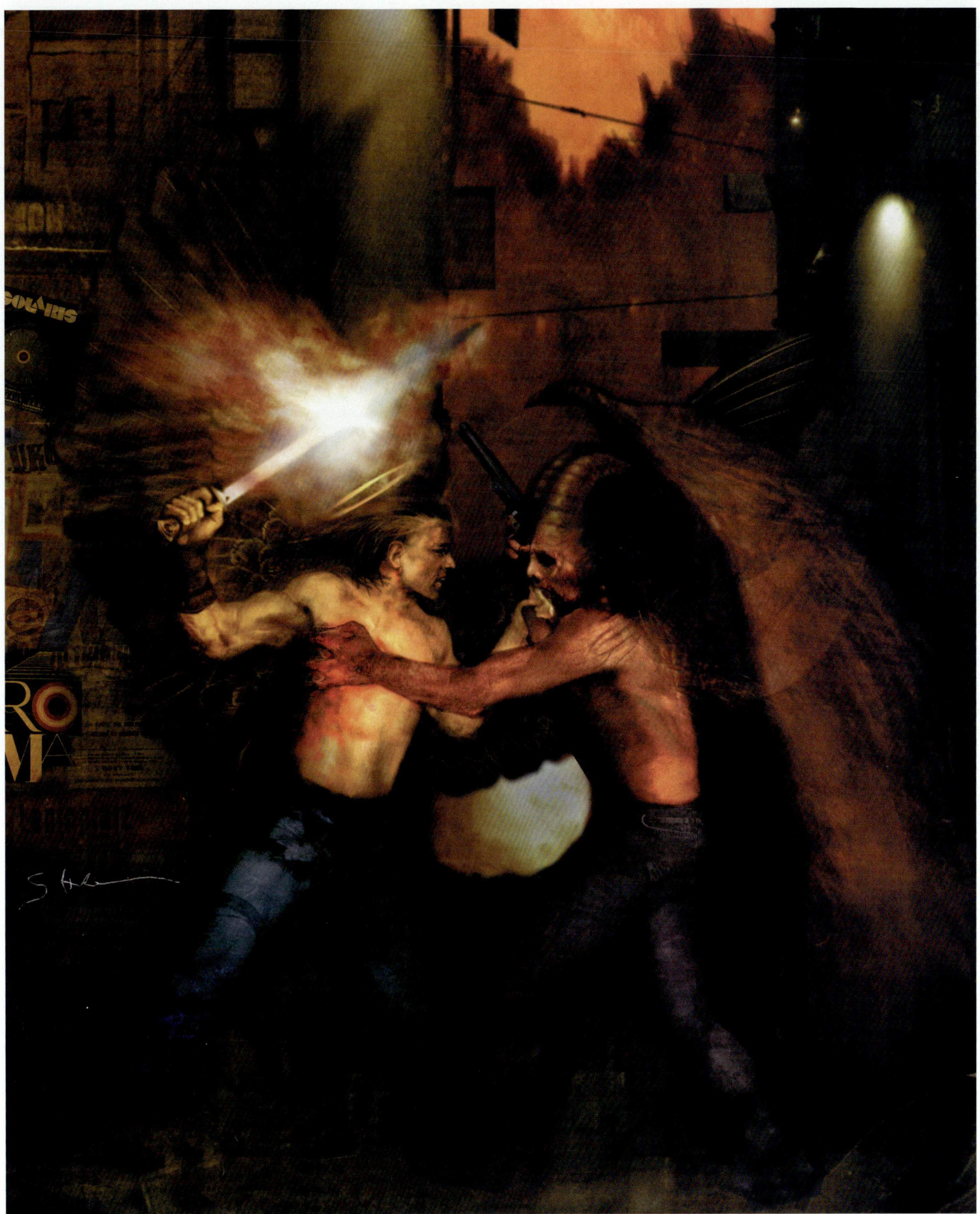

This cover has a history that is almost unbelievable. The painting on p. 8 was my first attempt at the idea of an angel and demon in combat. While the above painting was accepted and used on the hardcover reprint of Steve Jackson Games' **In Nomine** roleplaying game, I still feel the piece on p. 8 is a more dynamic and attractive cover. The art director from SJ Games assisted in the photo shoot at my studio so that we could be certain that this painting would capture the feel Steve was looking for.

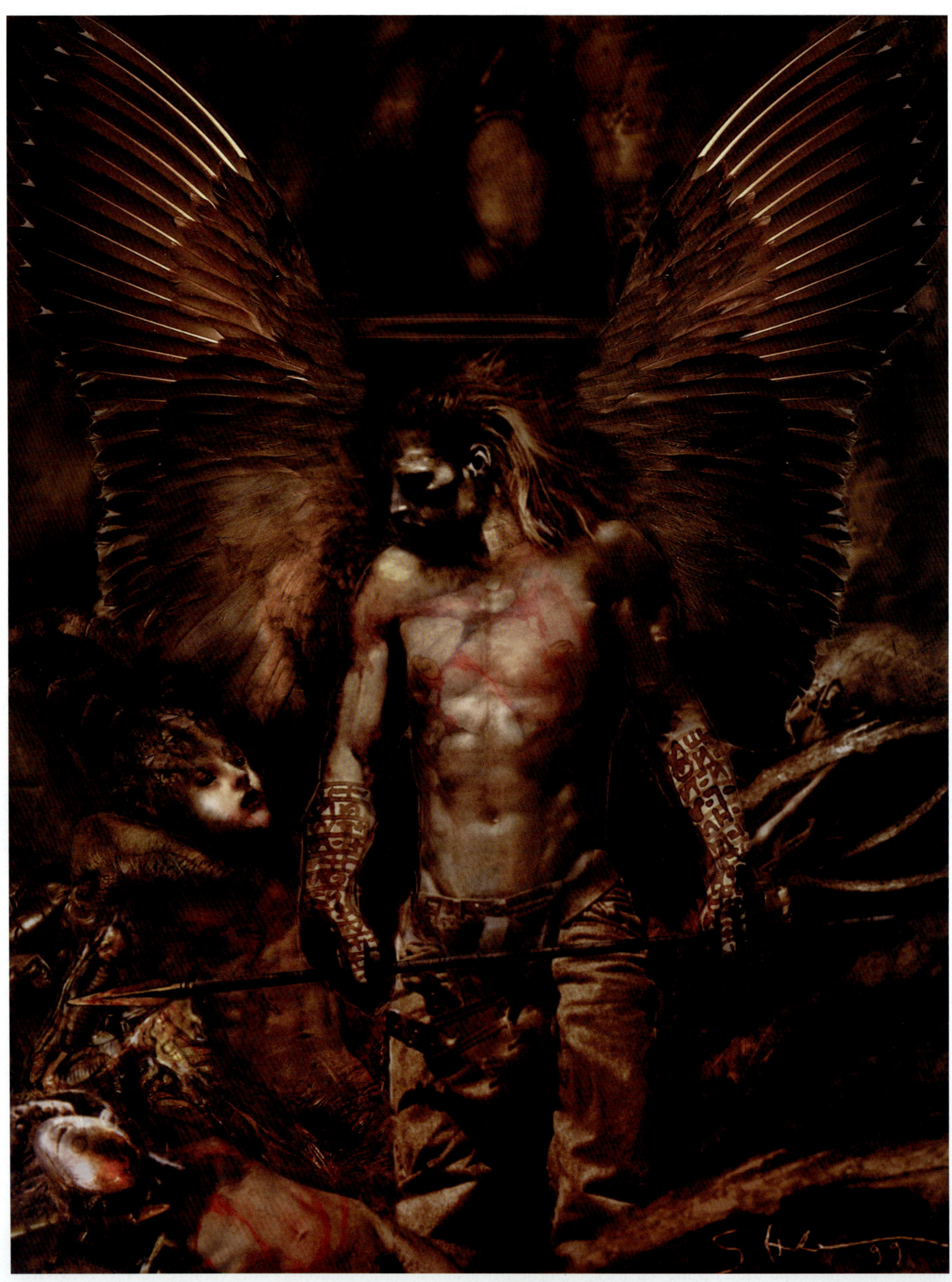

Another rejected *In Nomine* cover.

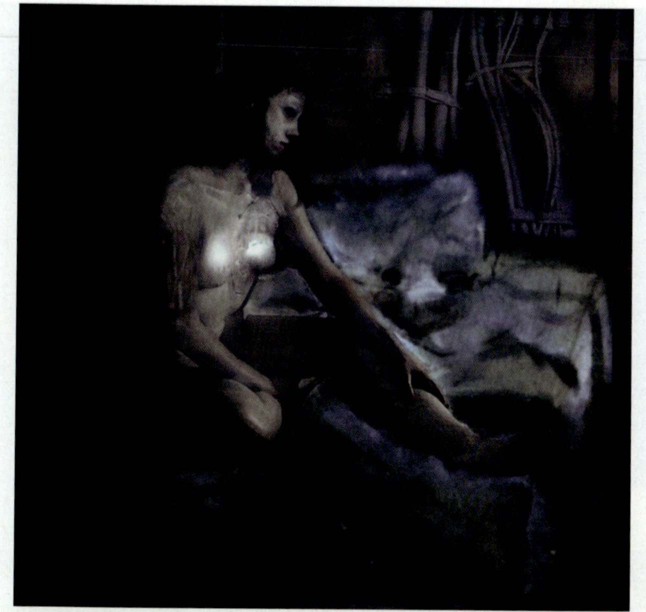
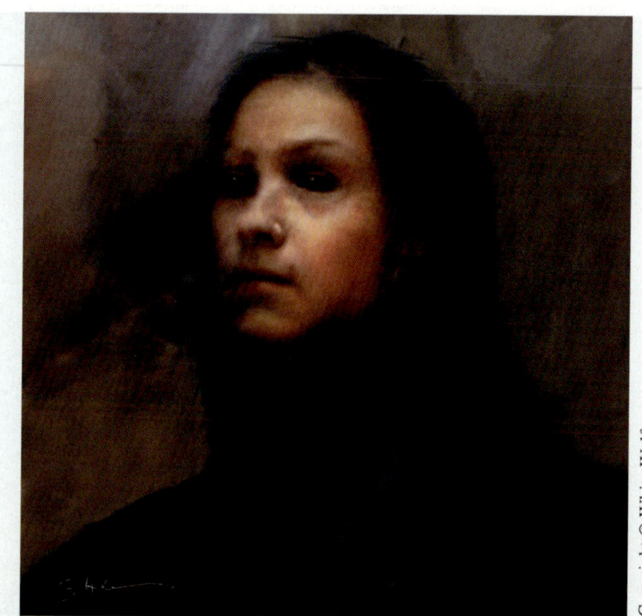

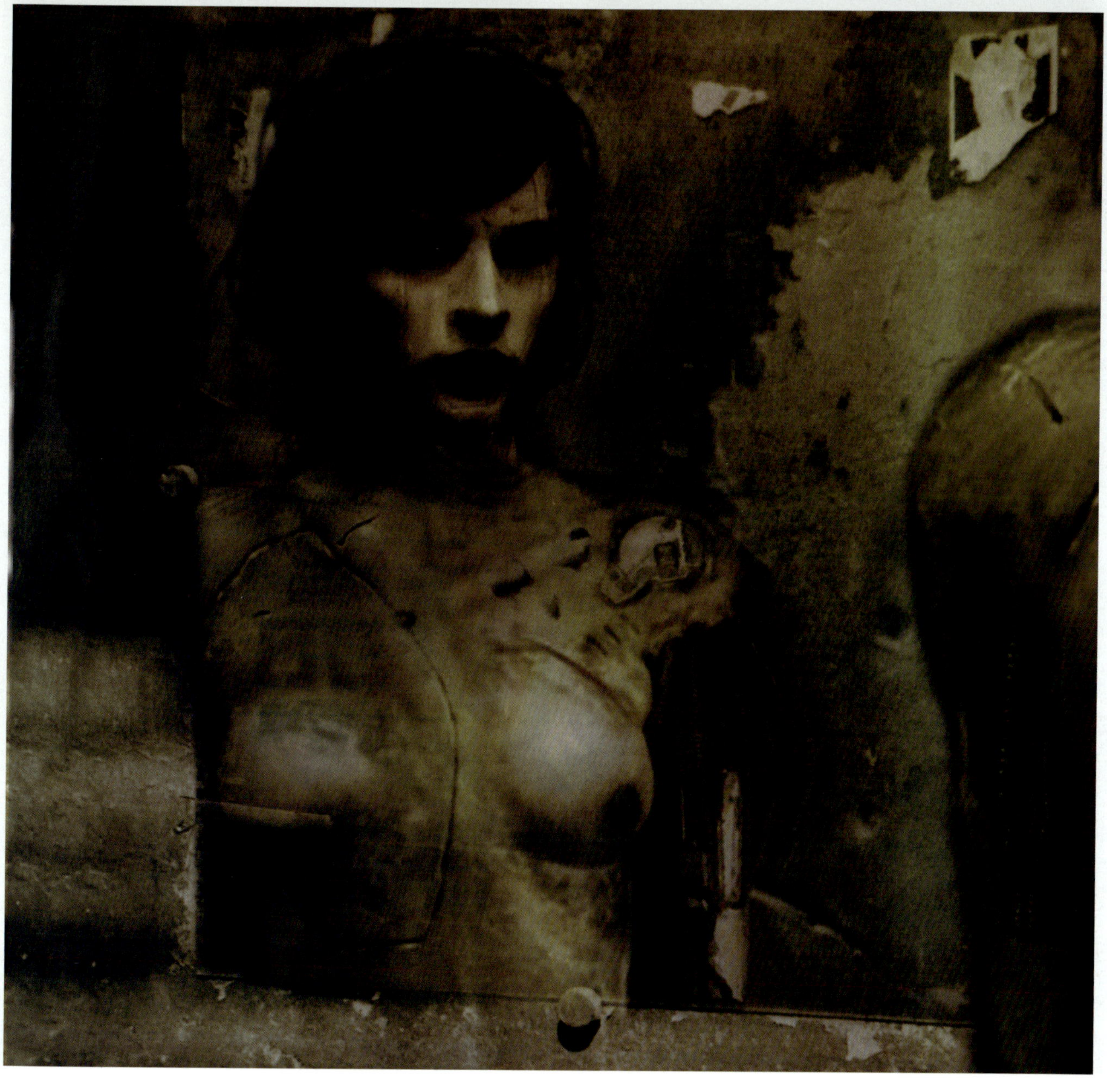

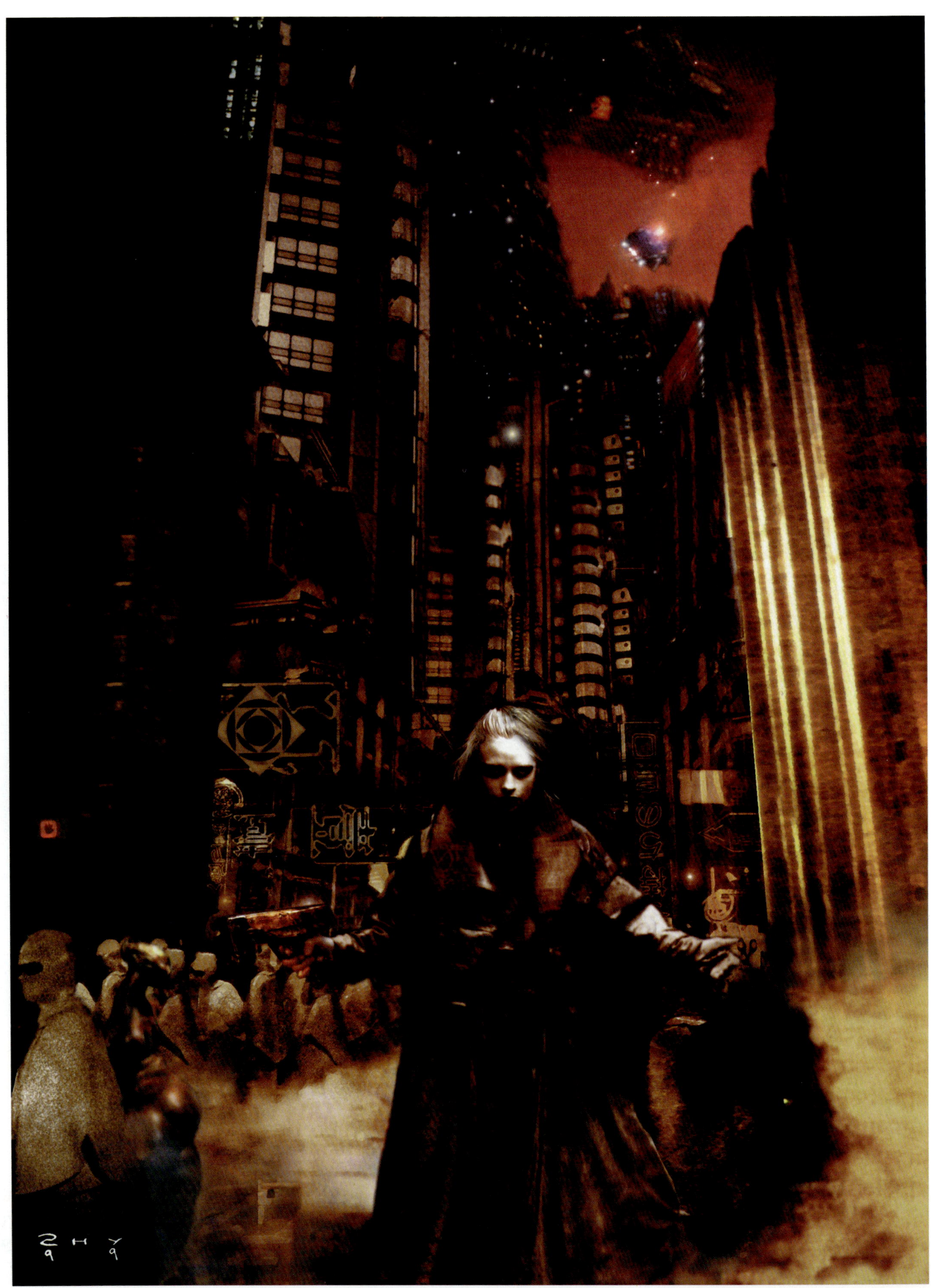

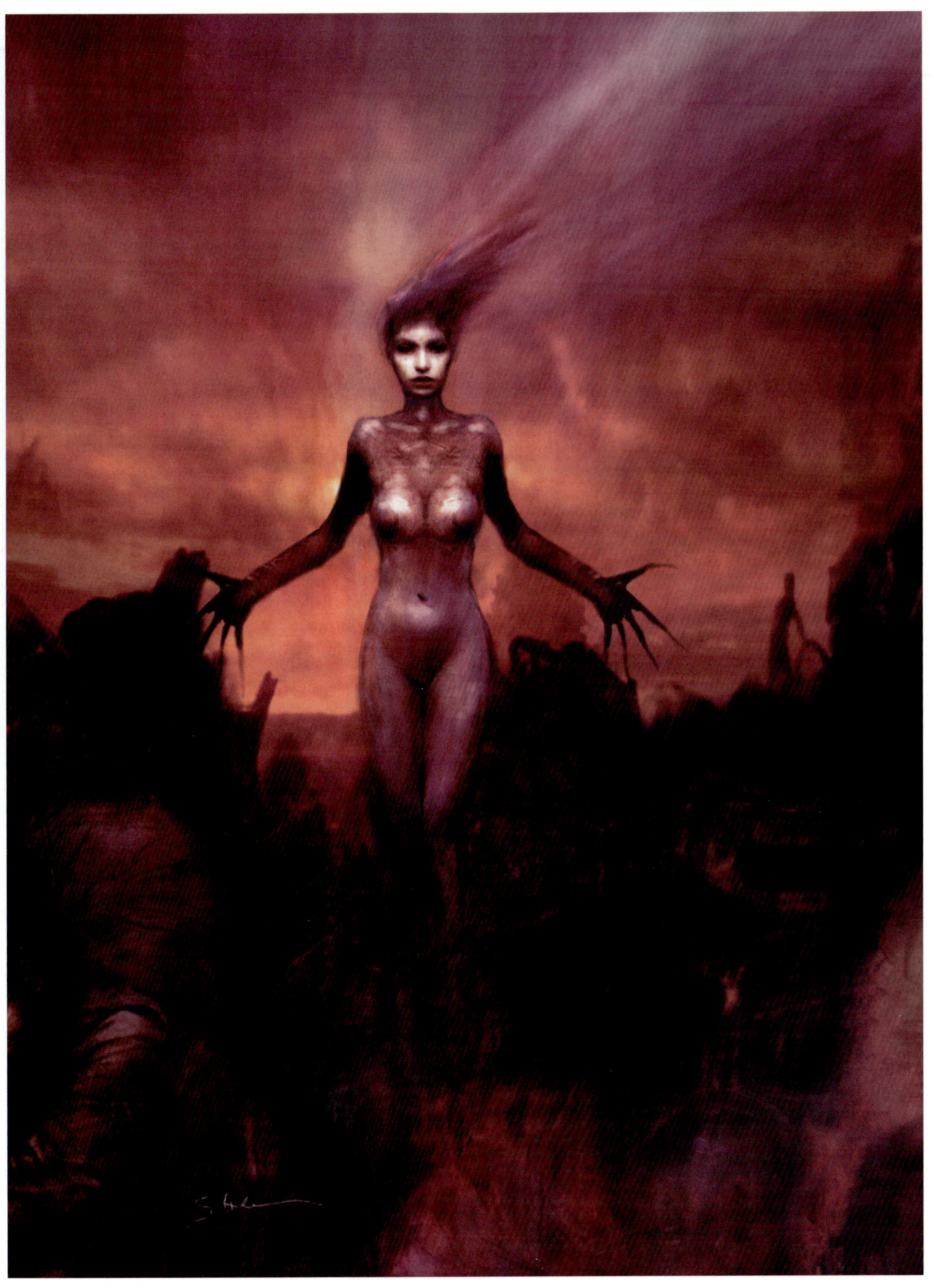

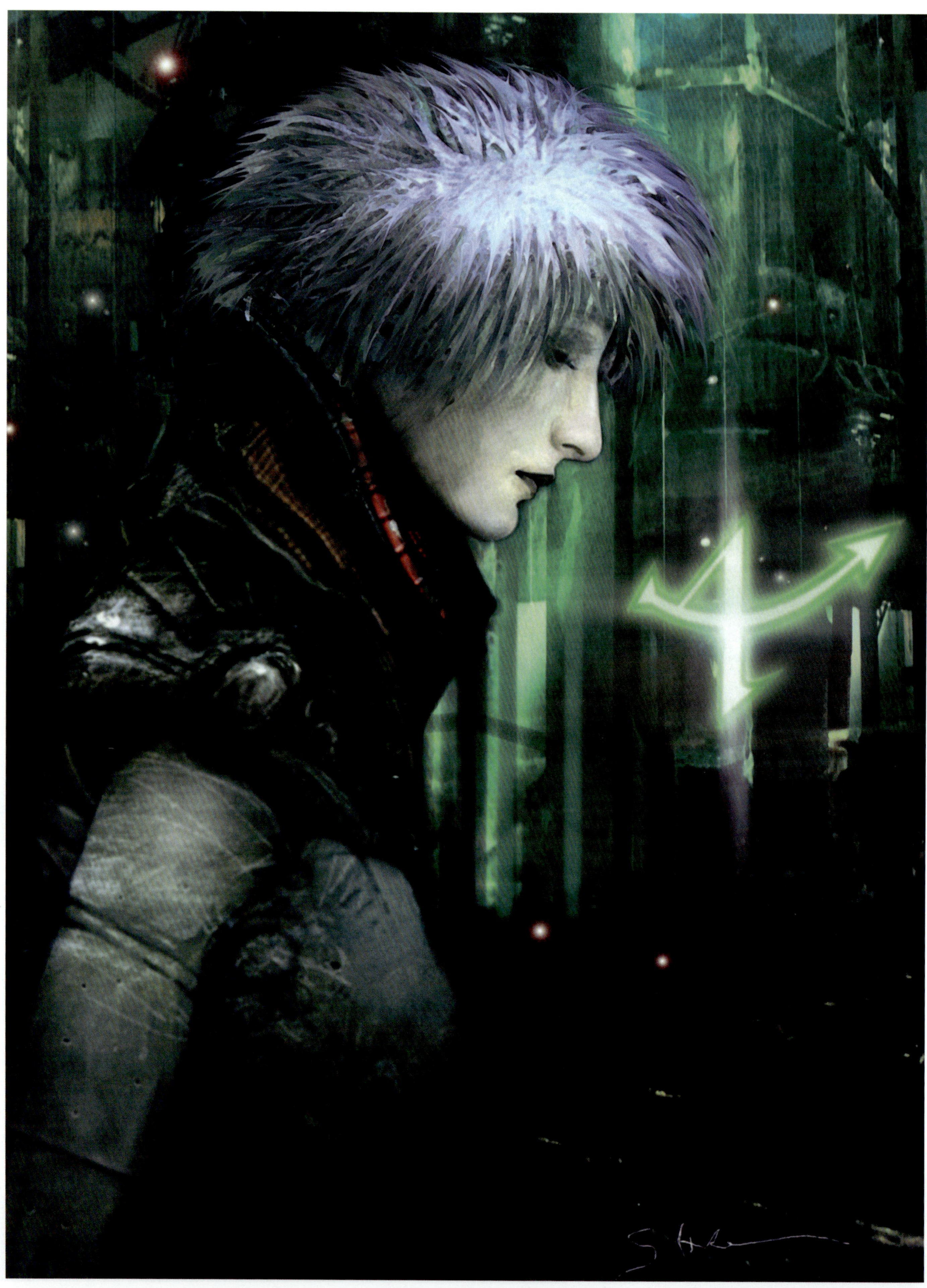

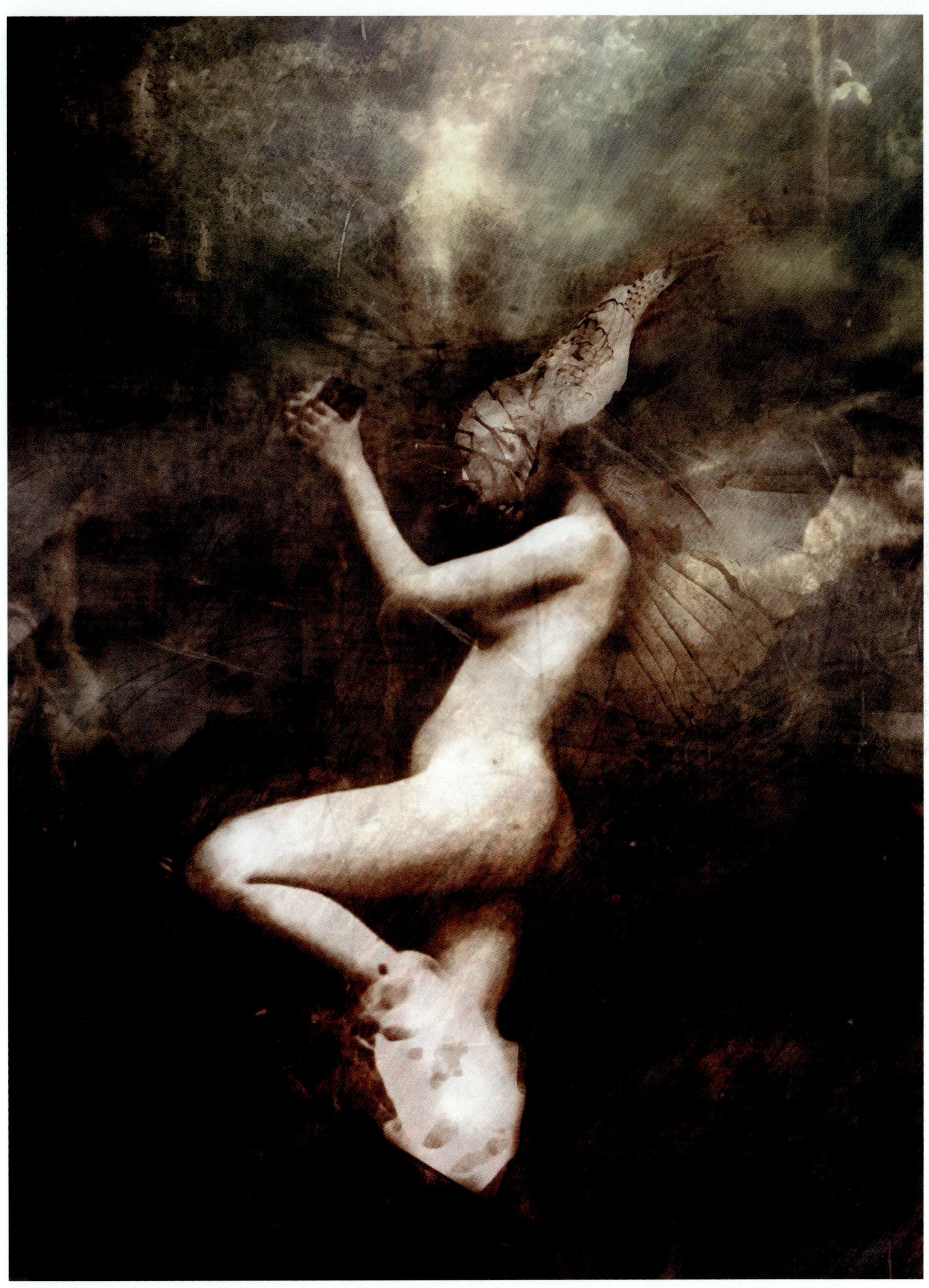

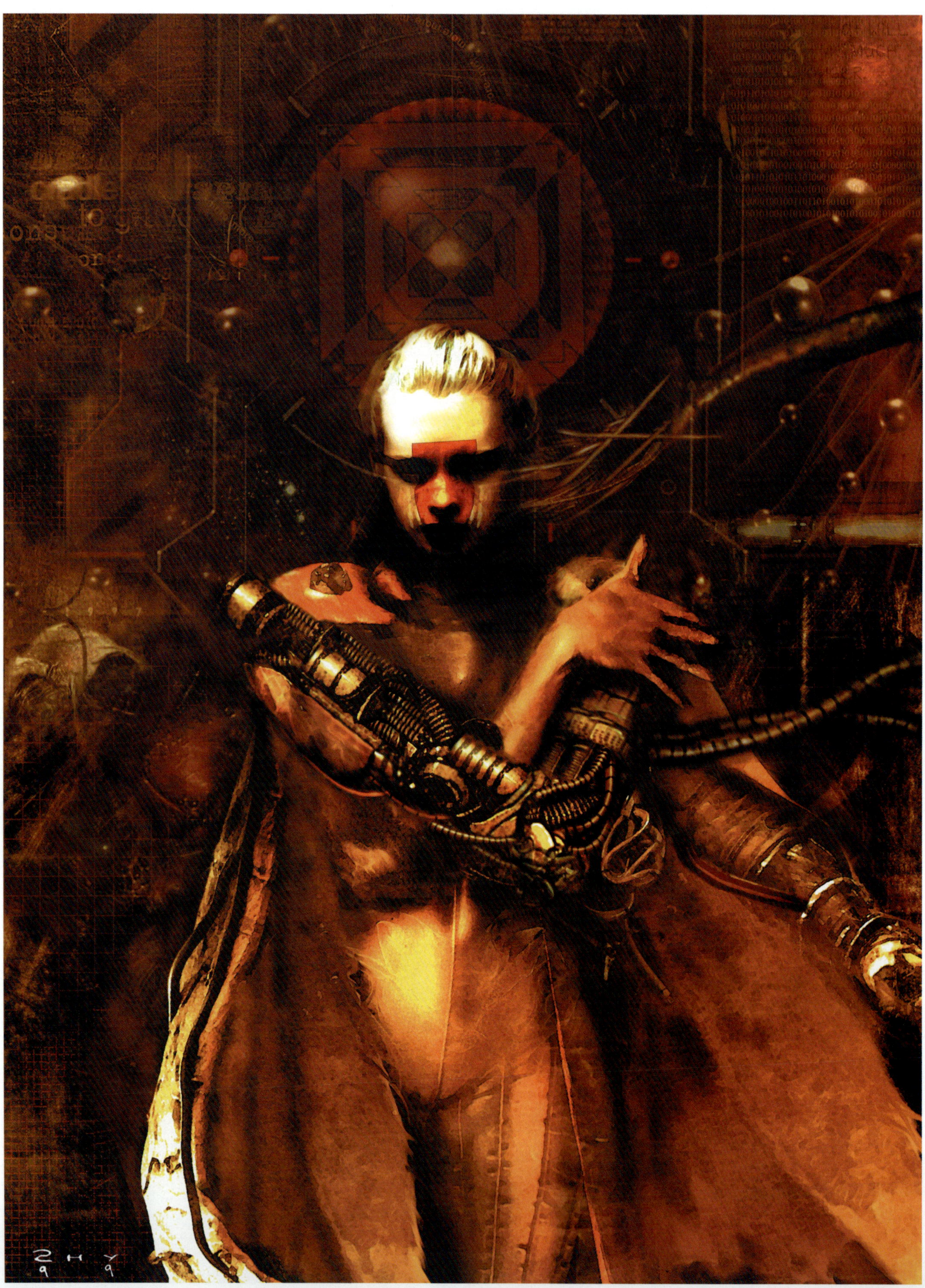

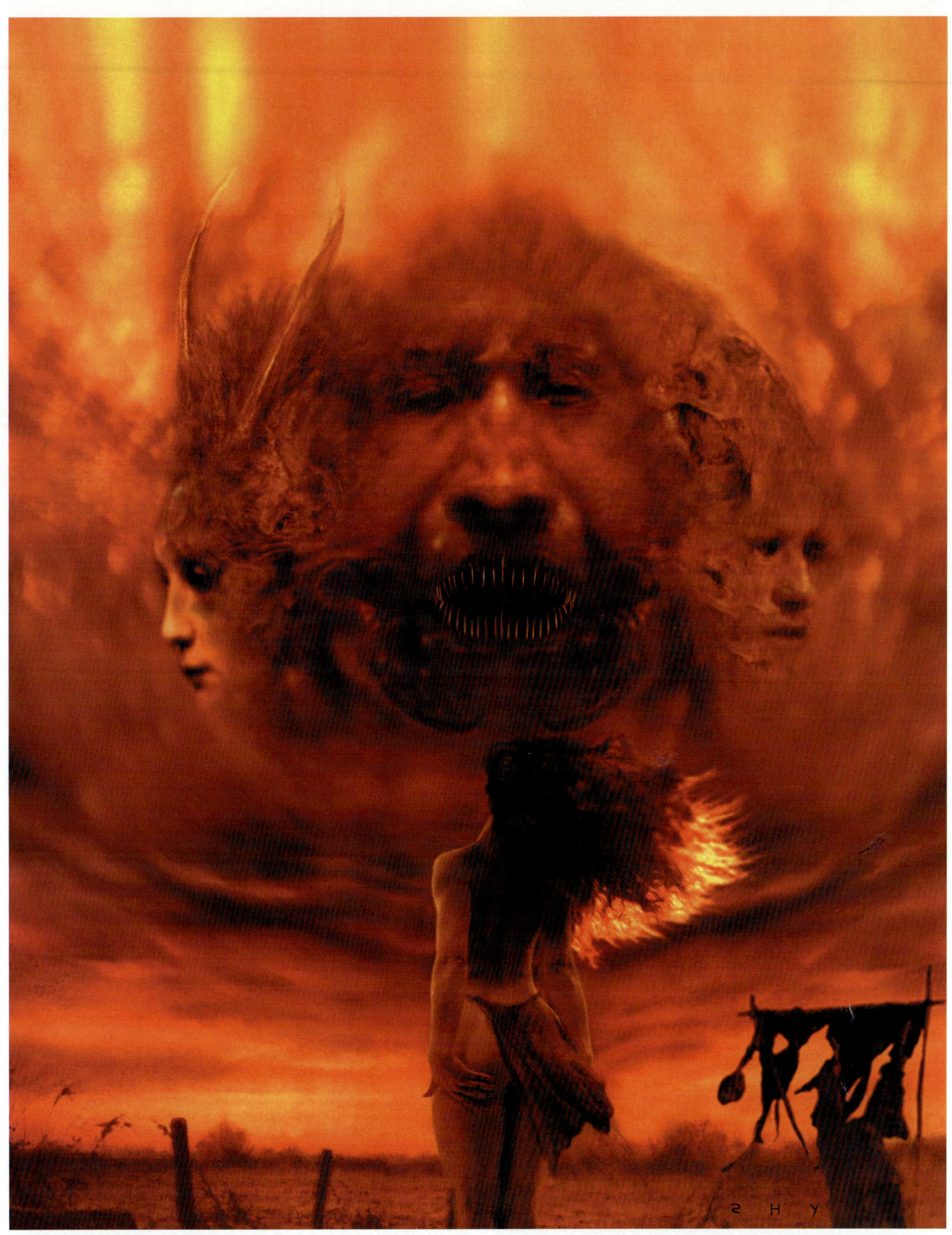

I spent New Year's 2000 in Paris, and saw things that made me lose more than a few sanity points. A Strange Moebiusesque world of phallic flaming headgear and strange circus animals being burned or blown up. This piece reminds me of that. The French scare me.

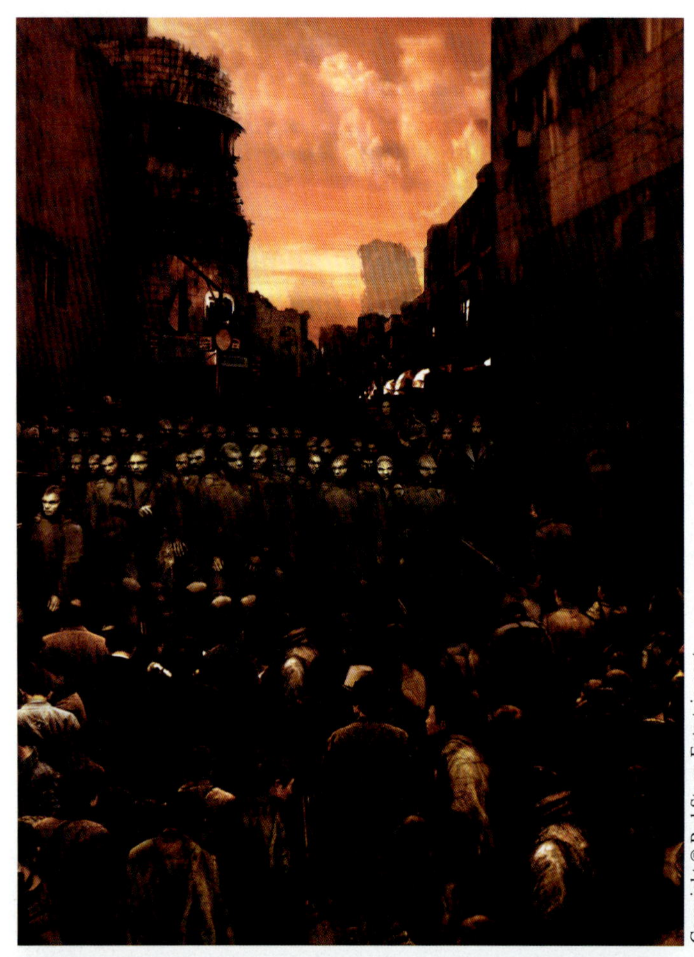

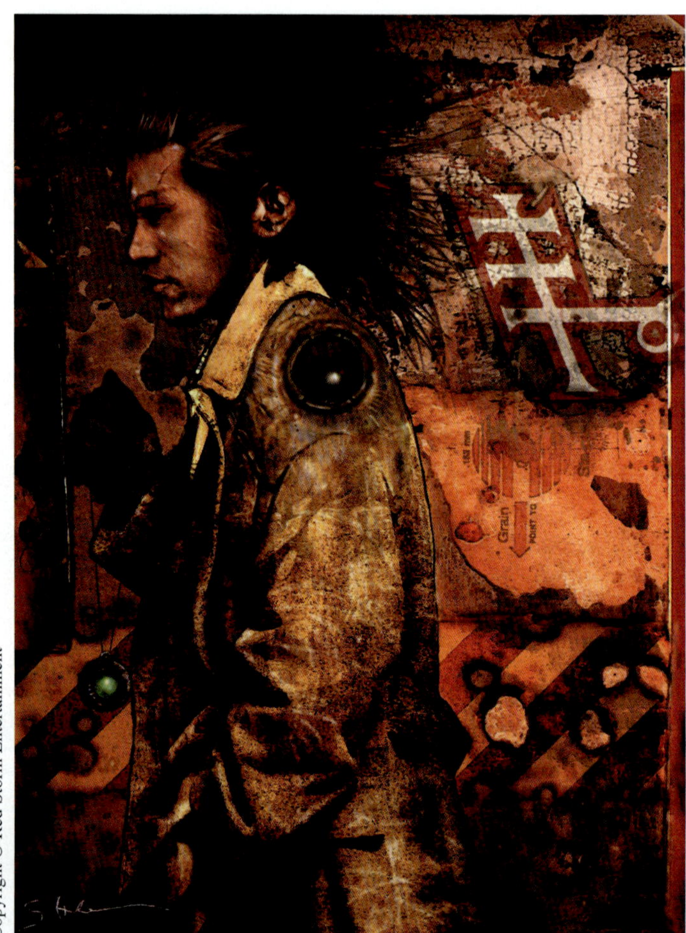

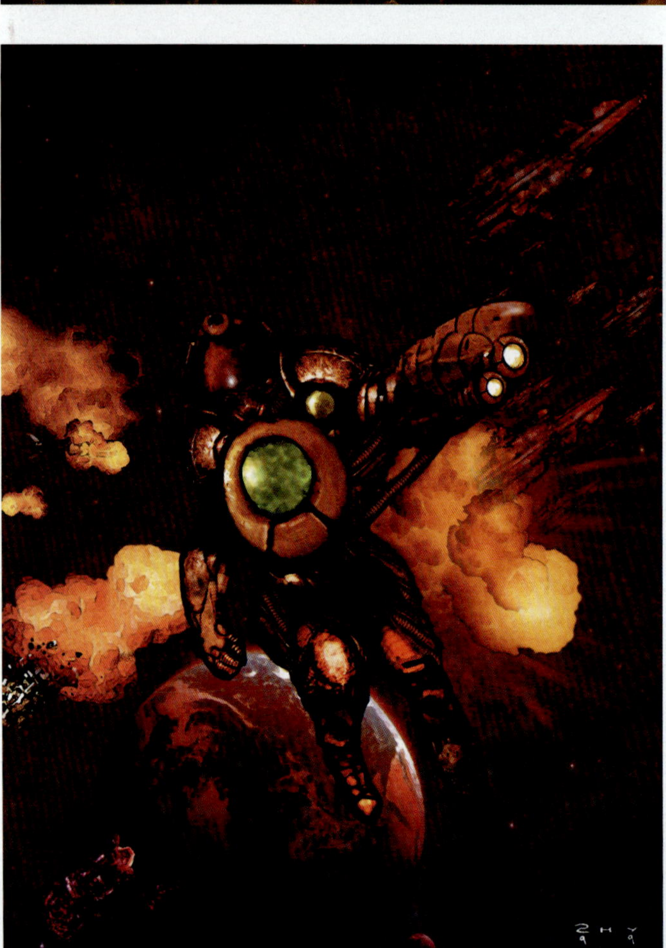

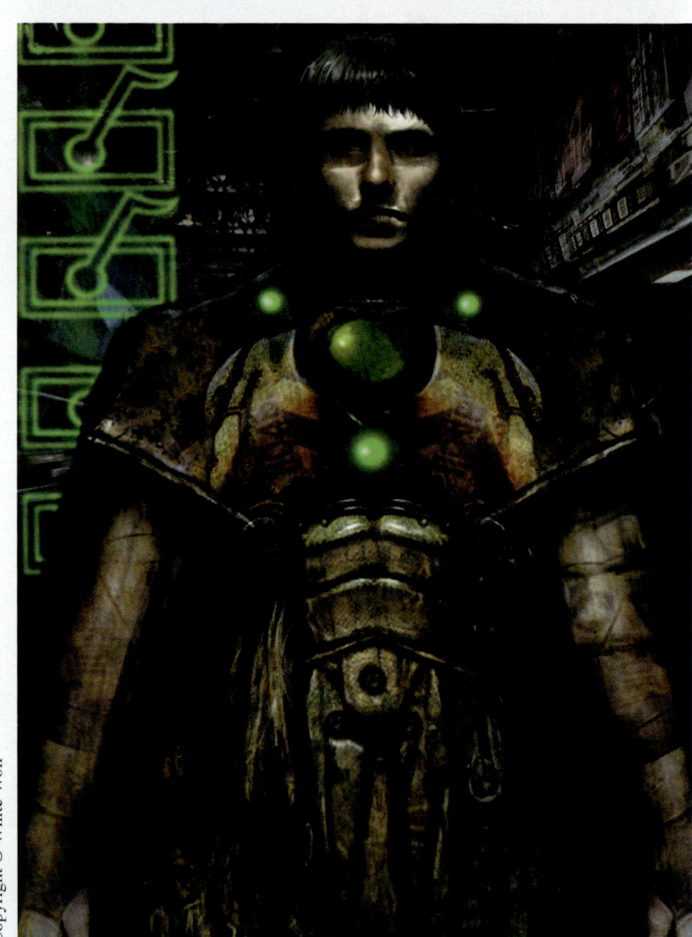

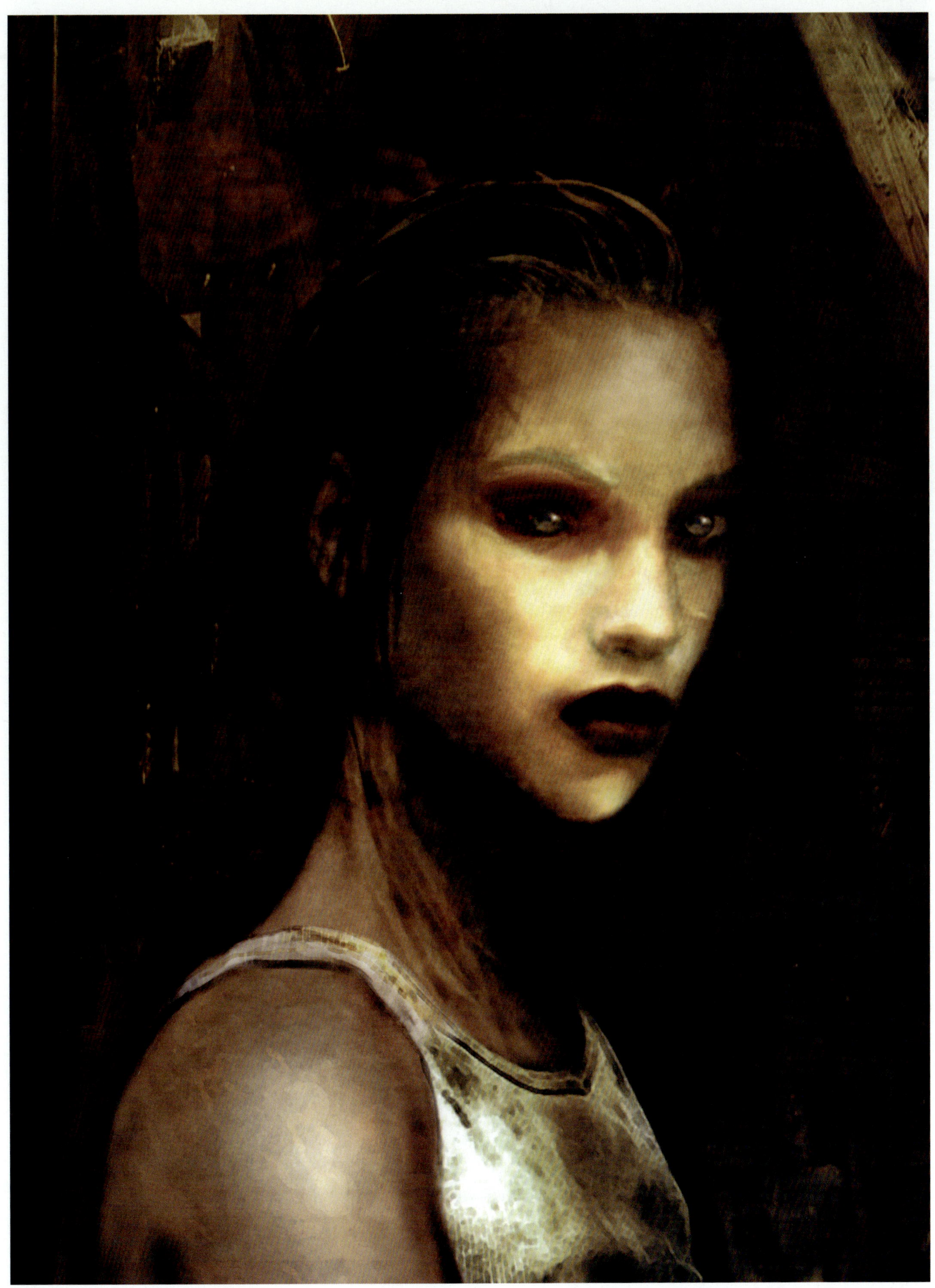

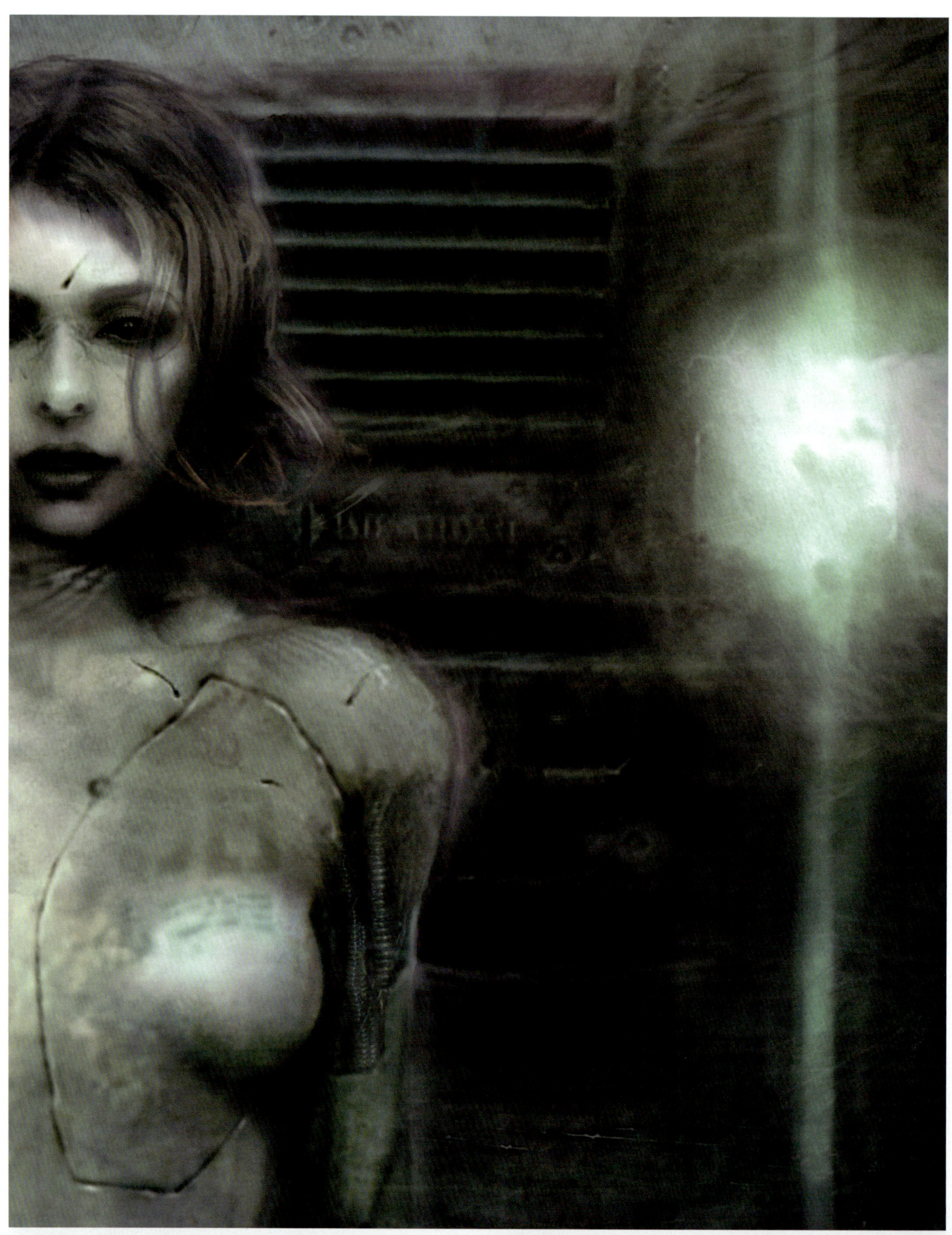

Concept work for *Man to Leaves*. Thanks, Jessica, for letting me ramble all night at Texpresso on this piece. I love the mood, and where it is was leading. I hope to start this series in the next year. Again, lots of smoke and fine line texture to bring it all together.

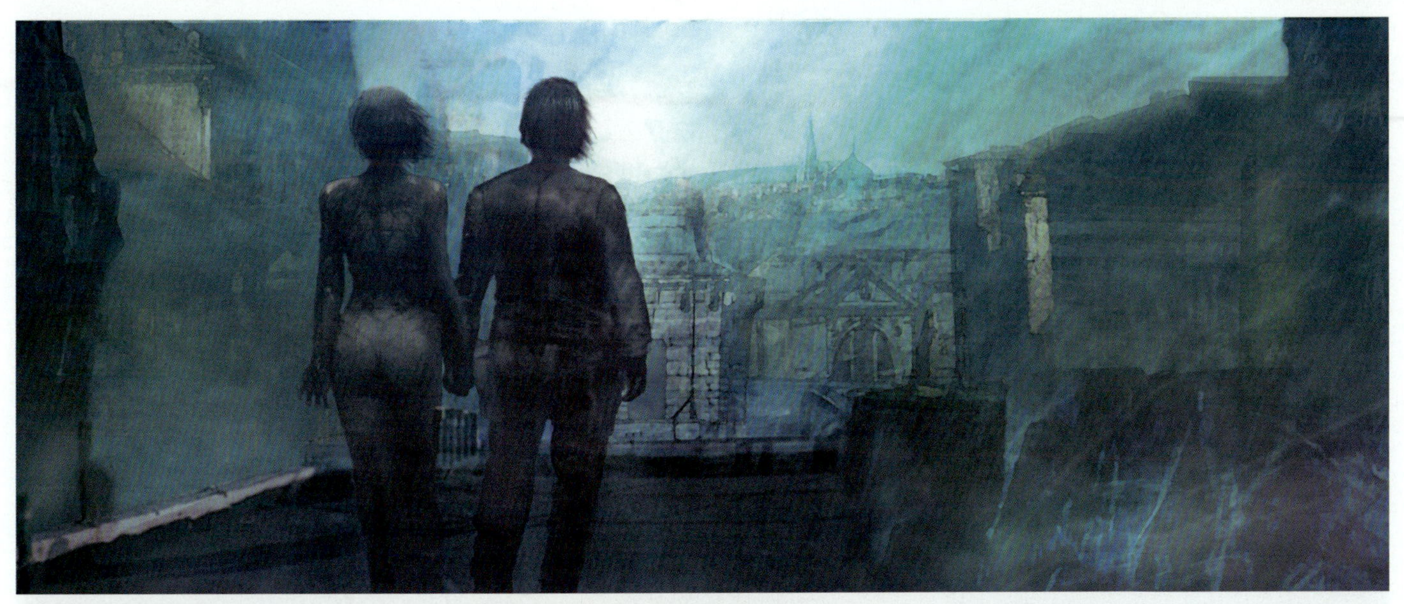

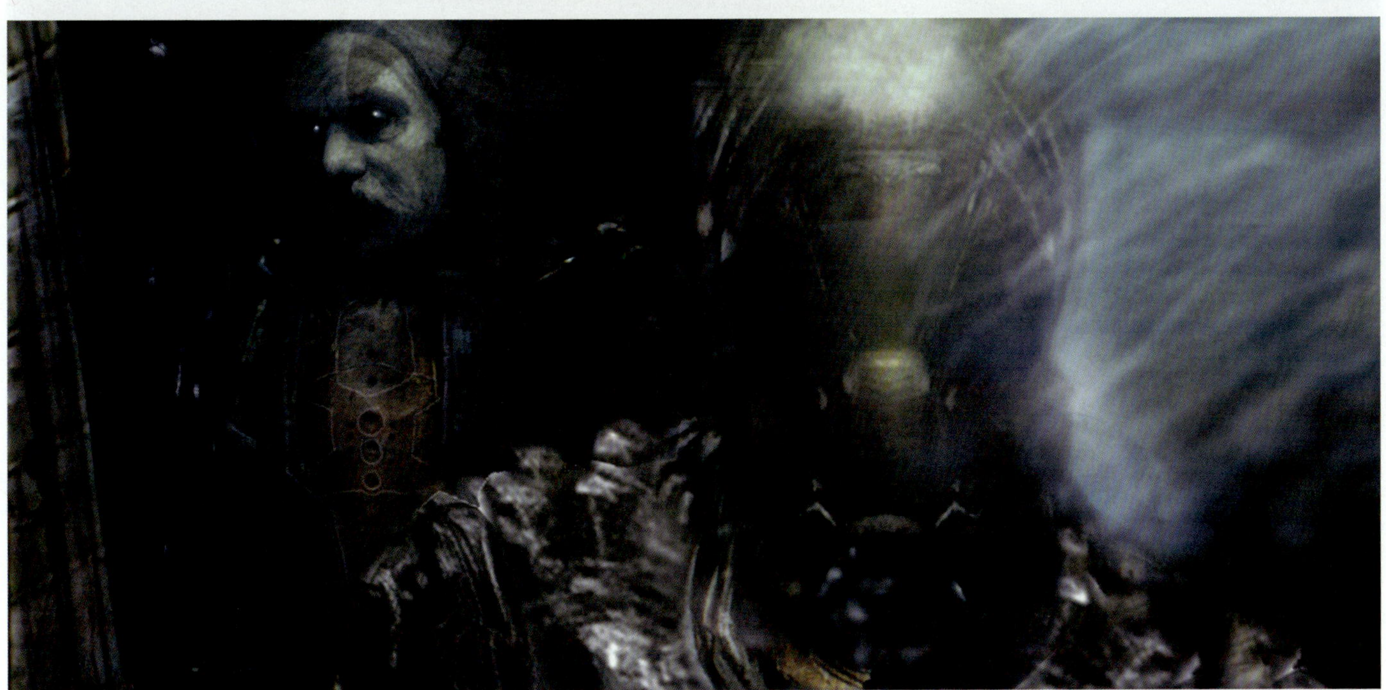

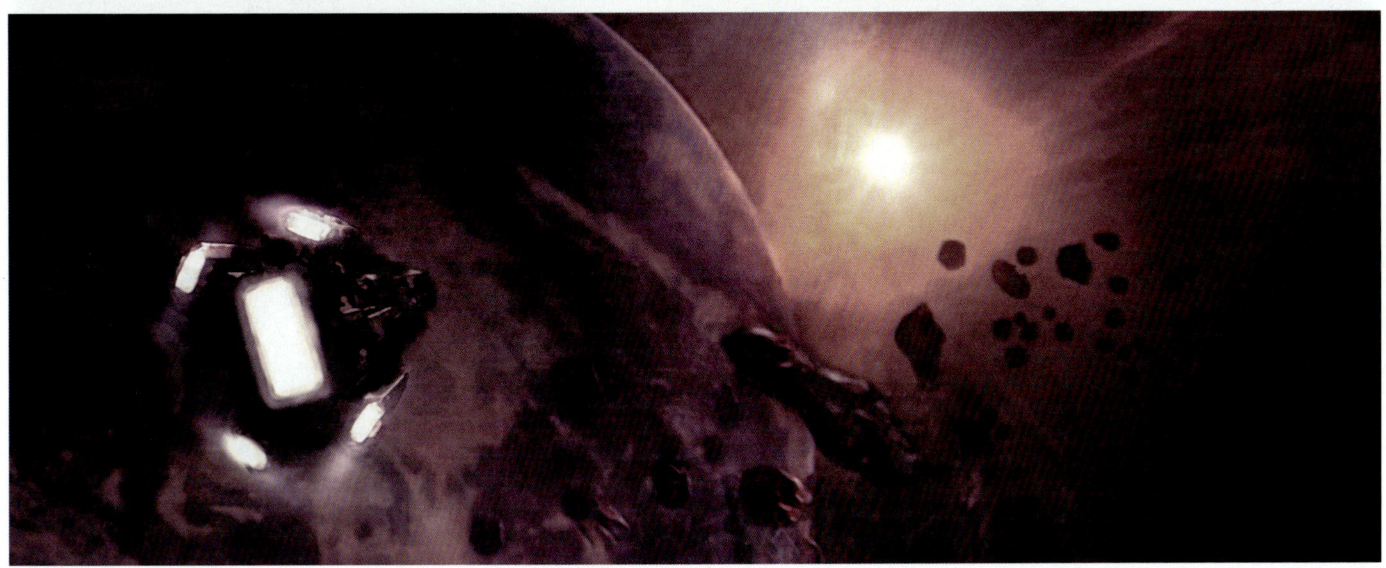

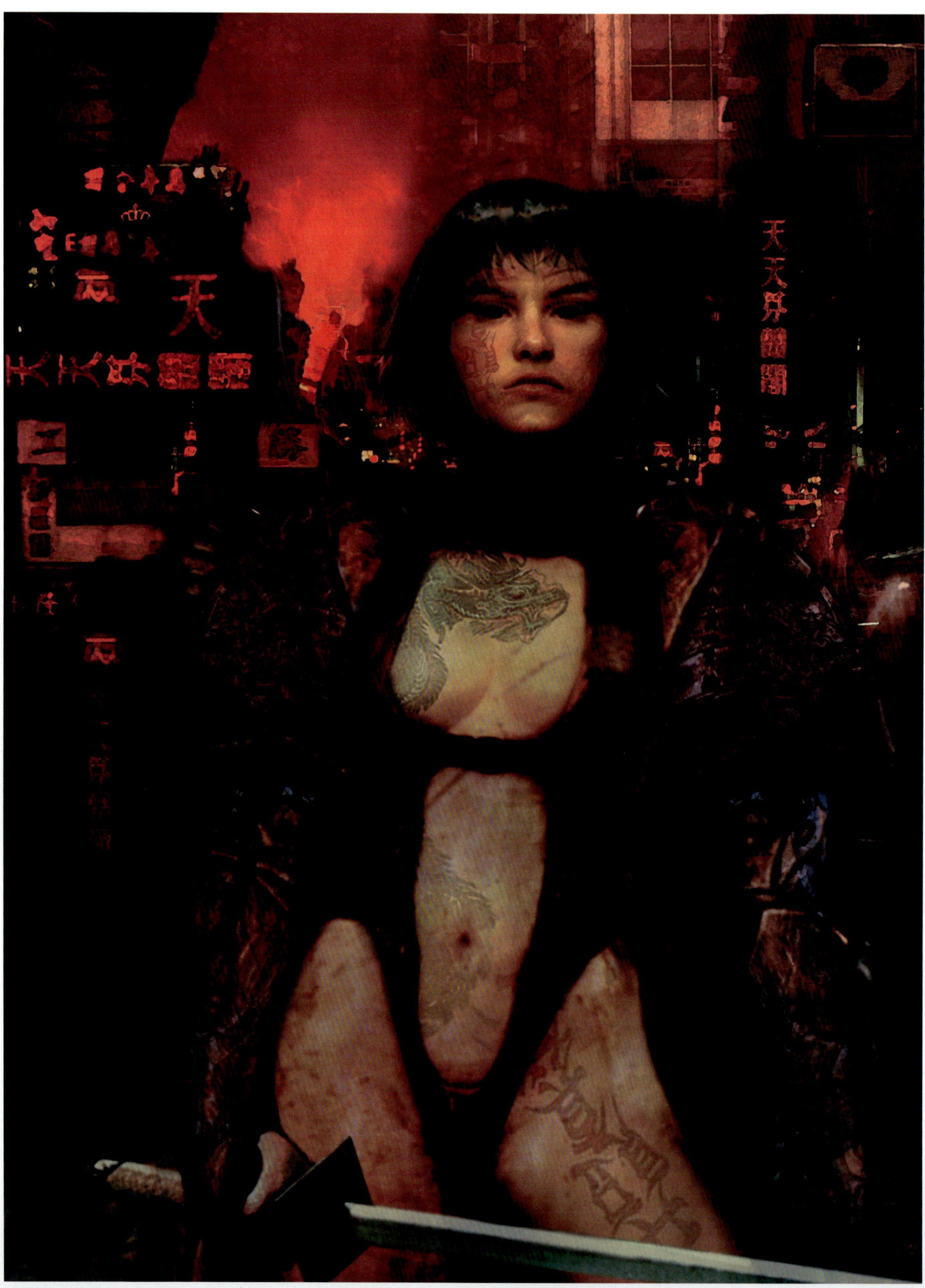

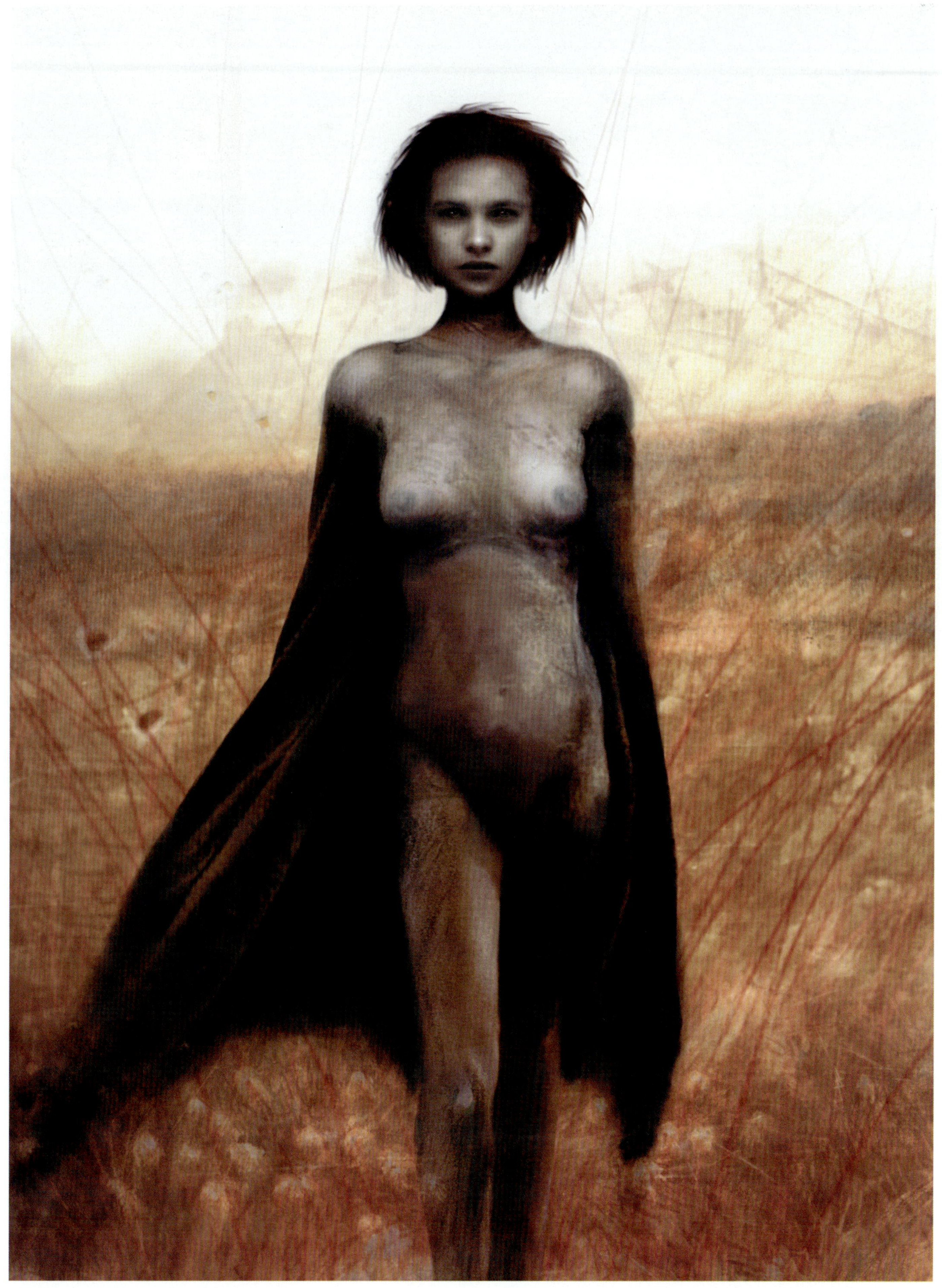

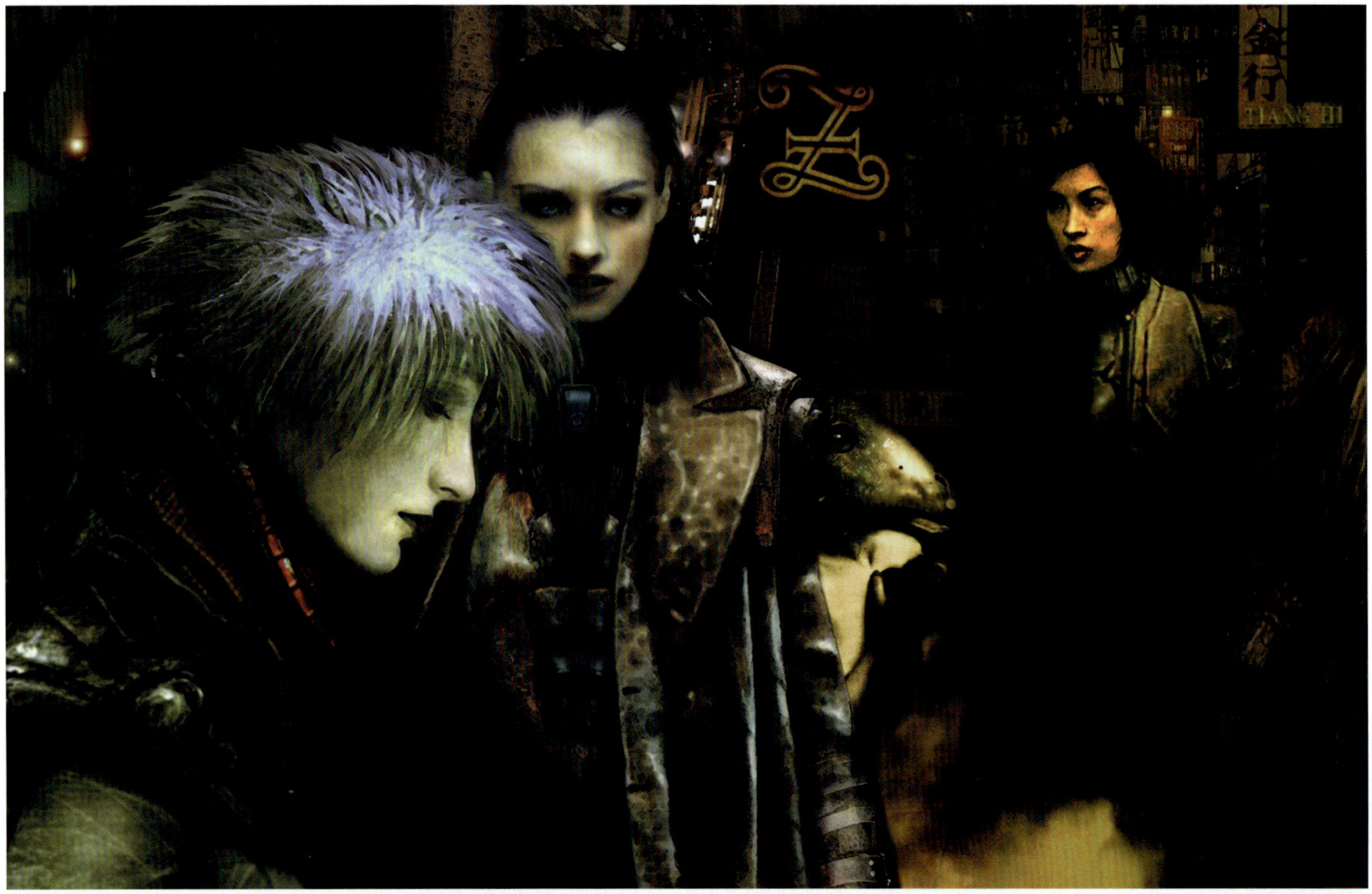

The finished *Mage* screen for White Wolf. It was very difficult working all of the individual screnes together and making it look fluid. I know Aileen and Rich had a stroke when some of this came in. I really do read the art notes, guys, but I sometimes experiment to a fault. I like to hybridize things together sometimes, bring in as

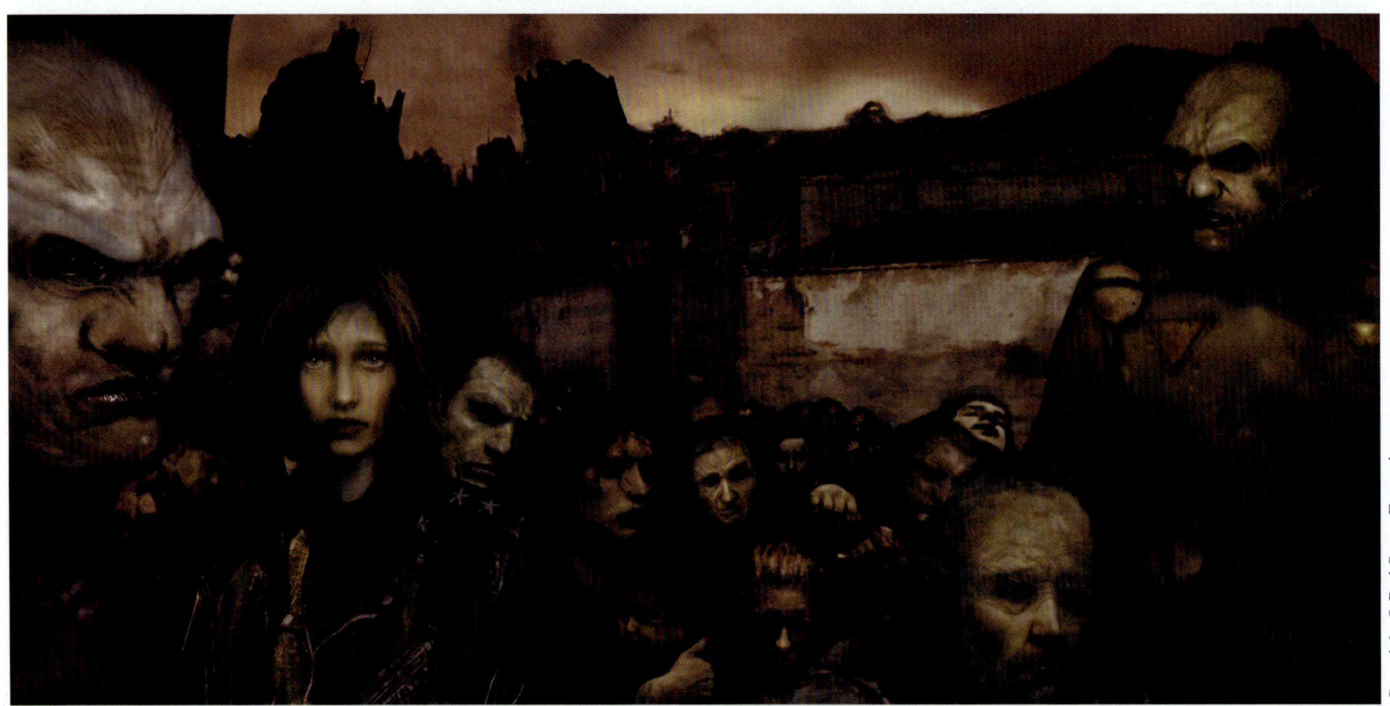

Some of the hardest work I have done. This was part of the intro animation for Red Storm Entertainment's *Freedom: First Resistance*. Special thanks to Mike Cosner and Steve Reid for being so patient as I learned

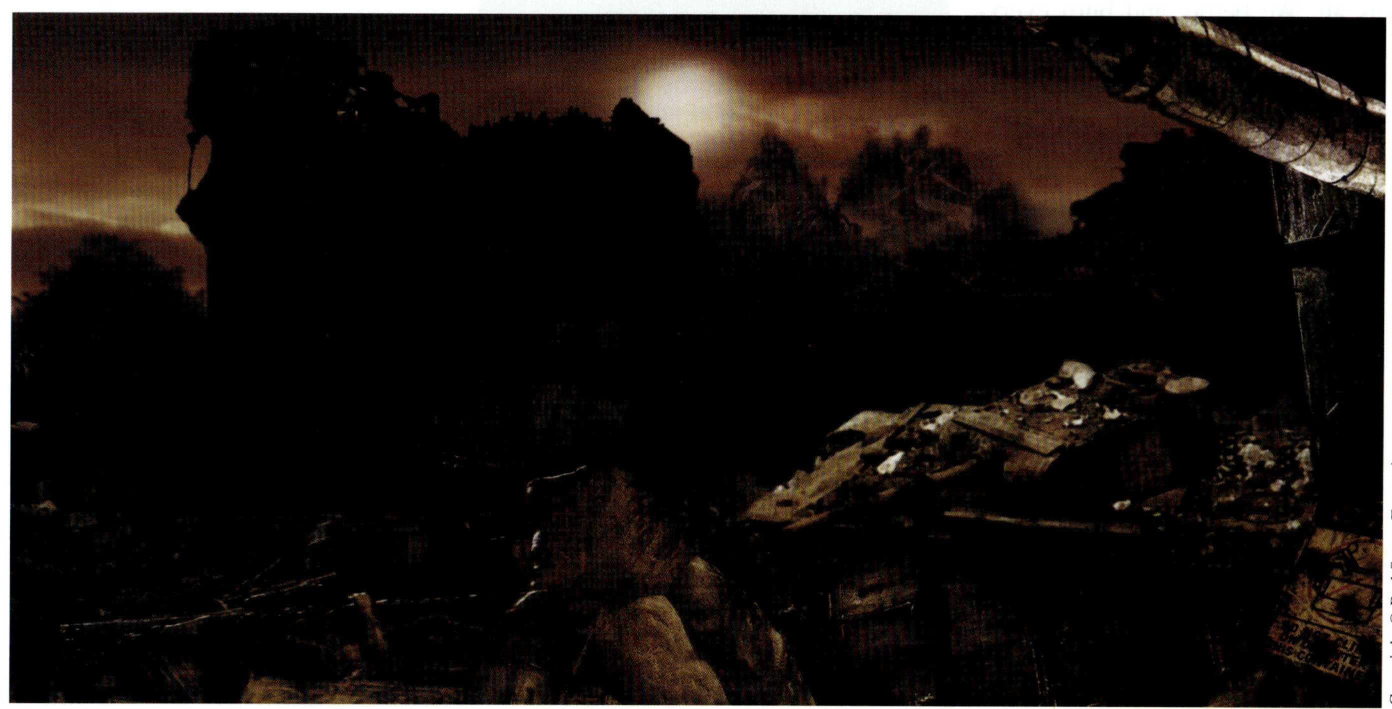

many influences as I can. I have gotten some flak over my interpretation of the **Mage** universe, saying that it was too futuristic, that my characters look too dark and techy. Rich and Ailien let me have my shot at it, and this is what I saw when I sat down to paint it.

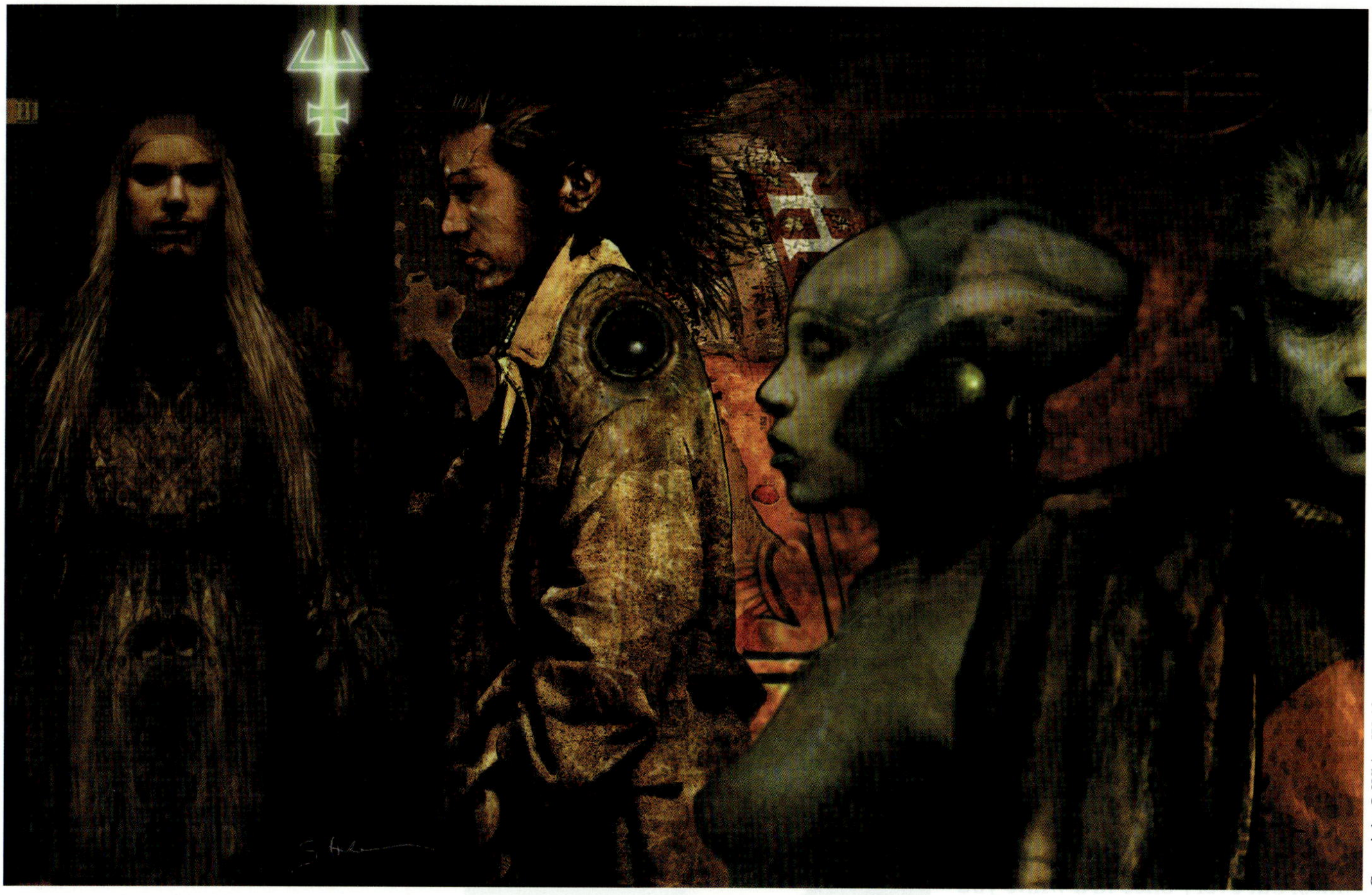

the ropes on this project. Both of these guys are brilliant artists and worked hard to translate what I was doing while preserving the detail. I have rarely worked with talent before. Thanks guys.